GW00399940

The Ti

My Life

-------- THE --------

'Speedy' Moore

---- STORY ----

JAMES McCLELLAND

Published by
Causeway Press
9 Ebrington Terrace,
Londonderry, BT47 1JS

***

The Times Of My Life
© 1994 James McClelland

ISBN 1 898787 07 7

● ● ●

Distributed by
AMBASSADOR PRODUCTIONS LTD.,
Providence House,
16 Hillview Avenue,
Belfast, BT5 6JR
Northern Ireland, UK.

Introduction

My first real meeting with Speedy Moore took place at about thirty thousand feet above the United States of America. I was on a flight from Atlanta, Georgia, to San Francisco, California.

This book had already been commissioned and although I'd heard about Speedy Moore, in fact, I'd heard a lot about him, I'd never actually met the man. So, to keep me company on the plane, and to acquaint me with the person I was to write about, I brought along his own book, *"Each day a new day."*

There are few people who could read the opening chapters of that book and not be moved. Speedy writes in a style that is both simple and fluid. I was tempted along, line by line, as the story unfolded, and almost upset each time I had to leave it down. The in flight movie was forgotten, the others passengers ignored, as I followed the compelling account of Speedy's life.

The transformation from a life lived for self and pleasure, to a life lived for the glory of God and the good of his fellow man, touched my own heart.

The amusing anecdotes, sometimes peppered with a modicum of exaggeration, brought many a smile to my mouth - and the odd chuckle, too, betimes.

A man who has lived so long and who has seen so much must still have many a tale to tell. So on a cold November morning in 1993, I found myself standing in the offices of the Coleraine Chronicle, asking for Mr. Speedy Moore.

Over coffee in Grandma Smyth's he began his story. Later, he took me up the narrow stairs to the attic archives of his newspaper office. There, surrounded by dusty copies of old newspapers, bound in black leather and neatly tooled with gold print, he continued the account of his long and adventure packed life. He told me about his childhood; his schooldays; his early introduction to the sport of angling, and the characters who lived in old Killowen, where he grew up.

In the measured tones and carefully constructed sentences which come from a lifetime of writing, he spoke with tenderness and unrestrained compassion, of his mother. She raised him almost single-handedly, after his father died when Speedy was just two years old. I could see, by the distant look in his eye, that he knew he owed her a great debt of gratitude.

I listened to him reminisce for an hour or more, and then it was time for us to say good-bye. But before I left he bid me God speed and wished me well with the book. "Write it in your own way," he told me. "Put your own stamp upon it. And feel free to draw from the books I've written."

As we parted he pressed a copy of his new cassette into my hands. On the drive home from Coleraine I popped it into the car stereo and was gently soothed by his renditions of the old gospel favourites.

"I must do this man justice," I thought. "I'll never have the opportunity to tell such a story again." I hope you enjoy the reading as much as I've enjoyed the writing.

James McClelland
January 1994

Chapter One

A CHILD IS BORN

The year 1912 will always be remembered in Ulster as the year of the *"Titanic"* disaster.

On the night of April 14th, that year, the great *"unsinkable"* liner struck an iceberg, in the chilly waters of the North Atlantic, off Newfoundland, and sank within hours. Fifteen hundred passengers lost their lives in the tragedy and the name, *"Titanic"* has been tainted with ignominy ever since.

Just about the time the country was reeling with the stunning news of the *"Titanic"* a young mother in Coleraine was breaking a happier news story to her family.

Mary Edith Moore and her husband, William, already had three daughters. Now a fourth child was expected. The baby wasn't due till the end of November, but already William Moore had decided that if this addition to their family was a boy, he would also be named William, after himself.

The news of another prospective addition to the family brought jubilation among relatives and friends. They began praying fervently that William Moore would indeed have a son and heir to carry his name for another generation.

A MOTHER'S THOUGHTS

As the bright daffodils of spring gave way to roses and sunflowers in the summer, Mary Edith thought often of the new life growing within her. She was a God fearing woman. Would the child within her womb grow up to respect and love her saviour? Would *he*, if she was blessed with a boy, bring honour and fame to the Moore name.

The summer roses faded and the autumn colours departed from the trees. Against the winter sky they stood as stark silhouettes, providing neither shelter from the winds nor a nesting place for birds. November came in cold and wintry. As the month progressed the cold began to bite even harder.

On his way to work every morning, at the railway company, William Moore blew into his hands to keep them warm. His breath was like smoke on the frosty air. Ice and snow were soon forecast and, as expected, they came with a vengeance. William and his other carting colleagues threw sand in front of the horse's hooves to stop them slipping on the icy ground.

INNOCENT CURIOSITY

William and Mary Edith Moore's other children, daughters - Etta, Jeanie and Annie had already been showing an innocent sense of curiosity about their mother's increasing size. In those days the stork was much talked about in relation to the birth of babies, but in the case of the Moore girls this answer wasn't sufficient. They wanted to know more and so, after conferring one with the other, they posed a number of awkward questions.

Mary Edith did her best to fob them off with plausible answers but when the time of her delivery drew near she arranged for the girls to be sent to a nearby hill, where they could enjoy the excitement of sleigh rides, till the stork had paid their mother his visit.

On such a suitable snowy afternoon, November 30th 1912, William, James, Cochrane, Parkhill Moore was born, at 44, Abbey Street, Coleraine.

For whatever reason, (perhaps there was little else to do of an afternoon in those days) several members of the family circle had gathered to await the arrival of the new baby. The infant was immediately made presentable and then passed around for each one to examine and approve.

At last it was the turn of Willie Parkhill, Mary Edith's younger brother. He took the child in his arms, waltzed it over to its mother and laid it gently in her loving arms. It is reported that W. 'Speedy' Moore greeted her with a wide grin. In the light of what his mother would mean to him as he grew up, it's fitting that this first smile was reserved for her.

In those days fathers were seldom present at the birth of their children. It wasn't considered a manly thing to do. Nor was it expected by most mothers. So, on the morning of 'Speedy's' birth William Moore had gone to his carting job with the railway, as usual. Whether he was sent for when the child was born, or whether he came home at his usual time we're not told. What we do know is that, when he arrived at 44, Abbey Street, he bounded up the stairs, an extra spring in his stride, eager to get his first glimpse of his son.

CONGRATULATIONS!

"'Tis a fine big wane, Willie." "'He's a big bouncing' broth o-a-boy." "He's as like you as two peas in a pod." "You can't deny that one, Willie." Such remarks as these from the assembled guests were just what Willie Moore wanted to hear. He was as proud as punch of his new son and enjoyed the moment of glory as, one by one, they pumped his hand and offered congratulations. Then, quick as he came, he was off across the fields, to the hillside where the girls were still frolicking in the snow.

"Mister Stork has brought you the gift of a wee baby brother," he called out to his daughters. They clapped their hands and jumped for joy at the news. Then, clasping daddy's hands and half walking, half slithering over the snow, they made their way back home for a first peep at their little brother. Their little hands were still half numb and their cheeks were rosy red from the cold night air when they peeped over the edge of the cot and studied the features of the infant who would grow up to be W. 'Speedy' Moore, their illustrious brother.

Perhaps it was then, when only innocent, childish eyes were looking, that the leprechauns gently opened the lips of this babe and sprinkled his tongue with blarney dust. Certainly, in years to come, many members of the family circle would stoutly maintain that's what happened. How else could he have been endowed with such a *"gift of the gab?"*

EARLY SORROW!

In 1912, life for working class families was tough. Speedy's father, a tall, lean built man, worked as a railway carter. He earned the princely sum of fourteen shillings a week for a life that Speedy refers to as, *"one of abject slavery."*

Alas, when Speedy was still an infant, his father fell seriously ill and passed away soon afterwards. Speedy's mother was left with four children, all of school age, and with no visible means of support. Back in those unenlightened days there were no state benefits. A woman in this situation had to make the best of it. It sounds blunt, cruel and unchristian. It often was.

Mary Edith Moore was, however, a woman of indomitable spirit and great courage. She very quickly adapted herself to her new circumstances and went about tackling them with determination. Right away she got a job charring. From early morning till late at night she cleaned and dusted for anyone who would give her employment. This meant that she and her children would, at least, have the bare necessities of life. These were hard times. That's simple enough to say but not so simple to understand. What it must have been like for this young woman, in these straitened circumstances, it is difficult to imagine.

Rising early every morning, summer and winter; setting out to walk to the homes where she would clean and dust; trudging back home again after a long day of physical labour; tending to the needs of her young family and then, at last, tumbling into bed herself for well earned sleep. And in all of this, no partner with whom to share her sorrows. No one to help her with the burdens she bore. Yet never once did she mention the hardship or relentless poverty she endured. Her personal pride kept her from bemoaning her situation and prevented her from seeking charity.

At long last Speedy's mother got a job in Gribbon's Linen Mill. This was a very definite step upwards. It meant steady employment and slightly better hours, although the days were still long and the work hard. At the same time she got a small house on the Strand Road, convenient to her work, so the whole family moved from Abbey Street to this new abode, and to a new life.

Mother now earned ten shillings a week. Four shillings went to pay the weekly rent on the house and the remaining six shillings had to pay for the food, the clothing and all the other necessities. Life still didn't provide too many luxuries in the Moore household.

OFF TO SCHOOL

Speedy was sent to school when he was just two years and eight months old. There was no one to look after him during the day, when his mother was working and his sisters were at school, so the education authorities agreed that he could sit beside his eldest sister, Etta.

When he reached the age of five Speedy was moved into the infant department, as it was called in those days. Very soon he had learned the alphabet and could count up to 100. However, as he admits himself, he soon lost his early enthusiasm for learning and turned out to be a *"very ordinary"* pupil.

There was in Speedy Moore, though, a talent, a latent talent, which at this stage in his young life neither he nor anyone else was aware of. This talent would manifest itself in years to come and make the name of Speedy Moore known far and wide. Thankfully, it would be encouraged by one of his schoolmasters, honed to perfection by diligent practice, and put to good use in adult life.

Chapter Two

HOMETOWN

The town of Coleraine, pleasantly situated on the banks of the river Bann, has a long and interesting history. Fifteen hundred years ago Ireland's patron saint, Patrick, was received in the area with gracious hospitality. He, of course, came not as a tourist to admire the scenery, but as a servant of God enquiring after the spiritual welfare of its people.

St. Patrick was offered a plot of ground to build a church and, it appears, was allowed to make his own choice of the spot. The place he cast his eyes upon was covered all over with ferns, but none-the-less, perhaps with some heavenly insight, he decided this would serve his purpose and a church was built. That decision of Patrick's also endowed the place with its name, Coleraine, from the native Irish language, Cuilrathain - "the ferny corner."

Even today, as you drive into Coleraine from the west side, along the edge of the Bann, the town has a certain old world charm about it. For myself, I'm always impressed by the view of the old bridge at night, with the floodlights sparkling on the sandstone and the reflection of the street-lamps dancing on the water.

Modern Coleraine has been referred to as "A Lady Among Towns." Speedy Moore would add, "With some justification!" He writes of his beloved birthplace:

"Beautifully situated where the broad sweep of the river Bann meanders to mix with the blue waters of the Atlantic, four miles north, the borough is convenient to *the world famous Giant's Causeway, the incomparable Glens of Antrim, six heavenly seaside resorts, and the finest coast road in Europe."*

And being a keen angler, Speedy can't help drawing your attention to the splendours of the salmon stock in the river Bann. Many an hour he's spent at the weir, a mile upstream from Coleraine, watching these spritely kings of the river sport themselves. They leap and dance in the fresh river water, probably shaking off the sea lice picked up on their journey across the Atlantic ocean. Then, with those mighty, threshing tails propelling them forward, they rush at the churning waters at the foot of the weir and leap towards its summit. Some make it at the first attempt. Others, for whatever reason, have to return again and again before they achieve their goal and swim further upstream in search of their native spawning ground. The miracle of nature, once witnessed, is never forgotten.

GROWING UP

Speedy Moore grew up on the Strand Road. That's the house they moved to when his mother went to work in Gribbon's Mill. Most families in the area earned their living at Gribbon's and the linen they produced was famed throughout the world. It graced the tables and smartened the beds of the rich and famous on the five continents.

When I say that Speedy grew up on the Strand Road, what I really mean is, that's where he ate and slept. Most of his time, when not at school, was spent in nearby Killowen Street which Speedy refers to as *"a magic place."* Perhaps there was more adventure and excitement further from home. Perhaps there were more children of his own age to play with. Or, perhaps it was the fact that Killowen Street ran alongside the west bank of the river Bann. I suspect it was the latter.

With such a well-stocked river as the Bann flowing only a few yards from where he lived, it's not surprising that young Speedy became an angler. He was just seven when he first stood by the river's bank and cast a line in hope of catching a fish. His first fishing tackle was stolen - the rod, a tapered hazel stick, cut from the Somerset estate - the line, a length of parcel twine, taken from a grocer's shop - and the hook, a stout pin from his mother's faded purple needle-cushion, bent to the required shape.

This primitive fishing tackle wasn't much use against the lively sea trout that jumped and played in the lower reaches of the Bann. It was pretty hopeless, too, against those mighty kings of the river, the salmon. But it was perfectly suitable for the silvery prey young Moore had his eyes on. Cuttings they were called, small sea fish that came into the Bann estuary every summer and yielded readily to a hook baited with bread or a small garden worm.

A favourite spot for catching these hard fighting little fish was a wide sheugh in Cameron's Marsh, directly opposite Killowen school and on the river shore.

A DIFFERENT AGE

Gribbon's factory horn broadcast its early morning alarm call across the sleepy neighbourhood at a quarter-to-six every day - except Sunday, of course. Long before that, Mrs. Moore was already up and about, seeing to her own breakfast, leaving clothes and shoes ready for her children, and packing lunches. Into Speedy's school-bag, every morning, went a large griddle-backed soda scone. Not very delicate provision - no appeal to those who were endowed with a sweet tooth - but good, sturdy Ulster packin', meant to stave off the pangs of hunger for a good part of the day.

Mary Edith Moore had no time to do anything else for her family in the mornings. That factory horn gave out a call that must be answered. Very soon the streets around the mill would be alive with the chatter of voices and the tramp of feet as hundreds of workers made their way towards another day's sweated toil.

It was a different age to the one we live in today. Employers were hard men and demanded much from their workers. Little excuse was needed by them to dispense with the labours of a man or woman and replace them with others more able or more willing.

The first horn blew at 5.30 A.M., the final one at 5.50 A.M. Work began at 6.00 A.M. and finished at 6.00 P.M. So, by the time that final horn blast died on the air, Speedy's mother had to be on her way. It was left to a kindly neighbour, Mrs. Tillie McGrotty, to make sure Speedy got to school for nine o'clock.

By the time the 12.30 lunch bell rang Speedy had managed to secretly nibble away the entire soda scone. For him, no thought of childish games in the playground. He was off behind the school wall, where he had hidden a spare fishing rod. Then it was down to that sheugh in Cameron's Marsh, to tempt those little fish he was so fond of.

The three o'clock bell signalled the end of another day's drudgery for the children. Before the bell had finished clanging, school-bags were stuffed with books, and there was a stampede for the door. The sudden surge of energy required to exit the school with such speed, and the first gulps of fresh air outside, reminded Speedy that, by this time, he was ravenously hungry.

However, the homes around Killowen were hospitable and generous. By the afternoon of almost every day a pot of home-made soup stood simmering on many a fireside. Speedy took it in turns to visit these kindly homes and to avail himself of the provision on hand. There's nothing better to revive the spirits, on a cold winter's day, than a steaming bowl of Ulster broth, with maybe a slice of loaf, or a bit of a scone, or a spud, dipped into it, to give it bulk.

LOCAL CHARACTERS

These foraging sorties to local homes brought Speedy into contact with a number of local characters - characters he feels should not be forgotten.

Tom Hemingway, a retired policeman, had the nickname *"Hooks and Hinges."* He served a delicious broth made from a pig's head. The pig's head was the essential ingredient on Tom's shopping list, at the town's market, every Saturday. All week long it was boiled in the big fireside pot, along with vegetables, lentils, peas and such like, to make that delicious broth Speedy was so fond of. Then, come the week-end, the well cooked, tender flesh was a tasty meal itself.

There were times when a lowly pig's head served the needs of more than one household. Neighbours, who couldn't afford to buy a whole head apiece, would have no hesitation in sharing its benefits, each, in turn, using the head to make a pot of tasty broth. In such simple ways were families kept together in body and soul and neighbours bonded together in friendship.

In circumstances not unlike those, a pig's head could, sometimes, become the centre piece in the most bizarre escapades.

JIMBO AND LIMBO

Take the case of Jimbo and Limbo, two ageing brothers who lived a few doors down the street from Tom Hemingway. Like Tom, the brothers took it in turn to go to the market on a Saturday morning to buy a pig's head for their weekly needs.

On one particular Saturday, Jimbo, whose turn it was to go on this vital errand, set off with the best of intentions. However, he, being like many of us, a weaker member of the human race, fell victim to the most insidious temptation. Jimbo was fond of a wee drop of the 'cratur,' and when a few old pals waylaid him on the way to the town and invited him in for a jar or two, he just couldn't say no. Furthermore, men like Jimbo can't go into a pub for just one drink. A combination of childish bravado and foolish pride prohibit that ever happening.

At six o'clock that night he was still there!

One drink had led to another; the crack had been great and, in the dreamy atmosphere created by the amber coloured spirit, the main purpose of his errand to town had been forgotten. Indeed, worse than that, the sixpence for the pig's head had been spent.

Eventually Jimbo managed to tear himself away from his friends at the bar and staggered home to face the wrath of his brother. What would they do for a whole week without a pot of pig's head broth?

Well, they managed to struggle through till the Tuesday, by which time hunger got the better of them. Since Jimbo had been the defaulter, he was the one who had to swallow his pride and do something about the predicament they were in.

When he stood at big Tom's door there was a pathetic look on his face. *"Tom,"* he lied, *"through sickness I couldn't get to the market on Saturday for a pig's head. Limbo and me were wondering if we could borrow yours for an hour or two to keep us in the land of the livin'?"*

Whether or not Tom knew Jimbo was lying we don't know. What we do know is that, without hesitation, he went to the fireside and lifted his pig's head out of the big pot. Giving it a quick wipe with a rag he handed it to Jimbo.

"I've enough broth to do me till tomorrow night, but be sure and bring it back then, for I've visitors coming on Thursday and would need to make a drop of fresh stuff for them."

Jimbo gave big Tom appropriate assurances and went off home singing the good Samaritan's praises. At least he and his brother would have something warm inside them for the next day or two.

"WHERE'S MY HEAD?"

Wednesday night came and there was no word of Jimbo coming back with the head. Tom wondered! Jimbo didn't turn up on Thursday either. When, by Friday morning there was still no sign of the pig's head, Tom, now a hungry man himself, went in search of it. He arrived at the door of the two brothers, demanding his precious culinary aid. Jimbo and Limbo brought him in, took him over to the fireside pot, and lifted out the remains of the head.

Recounting the event later Tom lamented, *"I would never lend those boys anything again. It had taken so much abuse I hardly recognised a feature on its face."*

THE MAYOR OF KILLOWEN!

Another memorable character from those days was Joe Tomb, the self styled, "Mayor of Killowen." If such an office had really existed there wouldn't have been a better man for the job. Joe was the epitome of sartorial excellence - bowler hat, striped trousers, frock coat and a butterfly collar with a cravat.

Joe kept five milking goats, Daisy, Fawn, Bridget, Pansy and Emma. Keeping them company was Joe's male goat, appropriately called Billy. Billy, apart from performing his essential male role, was a firm favourite with the locals and followed his master through the streets as he delivered milk from his female herd.

At the back of Joe's house there was a compound where he kept stray animals. It was quite usual for him to have sheep, donkeys, cattle, horses, dogs and even chickens, all in this private menagerie at the same time. Joe kept the animals there till the owners claimed them and when, eventually, they did, he charged them for the privilege, accordingly.

Joe had a big store of hay at the back of the compound. One day a local farmer's cattle broke into the place and gorged themselves with the hay, in fact, they ate every last bit of it. When Joe found out he was furious. He marched straight to the farmer's door and almost hammered it in. When the farmer appeared Joe got stuck in with his complaint.

"Your beasts broke into my shed and ate all my hay!" he roared.

"Was it good hay," the farmer enquired, quite civilly.

"It was the best sweet meadow hay in Ireland," Joe retorted, the anger rising all the while.

"*Well, what are you worried about then,*" answered the farmer, "*sure it'll do the beasts no harm.*"

THE PLAGUE

On another occasion Joe consulted the local vet for advice on a persistent problem. "*My heart's broken with a plaque of moths in the house,*" he lamented. "*Do you know of any sure way of getting rid of them?*"

"*Yes,*" said the vet, "*get yourself sixpence worth of moth-balls from the chemist. Your troubles will soon be over.*"

Next morning Joe looked tired and dishevelled and was in a rather crabbit mood. His eyes were swollen and red through lack of sleep but the vet ventured to ask him if he had tried the moth balls.

"*I did,*" said Joe sharply. "*I've been up all night and never hit one blinkin' moth.*"

Chapter Three

THE TRAMP POET

It's amazing how the most unlikely circumstances can throw up the most unusual and interesting characters.

Such a character was "Dusty Rhodes" the tramp.

To call him a tramp seems hardly fair for he deserved the title only because, for most of his life, he had no fixed abode. Despite that, he travelled the world, from his birthplace in North Antrim to the gold fields of California, and a lot of places in between.

He wasn't a tramp in the sense of being a beggar either. Dusty's needs were small. A bite to eat and the clothes he wore were sufficient for his daily needs. Even these were paid for out of his own pocket, indeed his own earnings, for in his own way, Dusty was an entrepreneur.

His proper name was James Stoddard Moore and he was born in Cushendall. His father was of humble stock and came from Stob's Green, Edinburgh. His mother, Catherine, was the daughter of Patrick Graham, a local small farmer. James was their only child.

He was born in an old corn mill, on Christmas day 1844. The name "Dusty Rhodes," he took to himself as a pen name, for his main claim to fame was his poetry.

"Twas a beautiful day in summer,
Bright flowers begemmed the valley

Beside a bubbling fountain
In the valley where I lay.
The song birds sweetly carolled
Through the verdant woodland alley,
When high above the tree tops
Shone the glorious God of day."

That poem *"The Penitent's Dream,"* was written when Dusty was about fourteen years old. His mother and father had just died - taken away suddenly by a fever that swept the little town of Cushendall.

Any learning Dusty had acquired had come from his father, so his sudden death was an even greater blow to the young lad. Despite having little opportunity for education, Dusty showed good intelligence and a love for poetry. He also read a lot and in due course began composing his own rhyme.

These poems were eventually printed in leaflet form and many of them were printed in northern papers, like the Coleraine Chronicle and the Northern Constitution. Dusty made a few shillings by selling them round the doors too.

IN SEARCH OF ADVENTURE

When he was fifteen the call of the sea and the thirst for adventure brought an itch to his feet. He turned his back on his native Cushendall and headed for the great city of Liverpool, then, even more than now, a Mecca for shipping. In those days when ships left the quiet shores of the Mersey and faced the choppy waters of the Irish sea, they followed all points of the compass to destinations near and far.

Dusty's first job was as a cabin boy on the barque *"St. Dominic,"* transporting general cargo to San Francisco. What a thrill it must have been for a lad of fifteen years to sail in through that magnificent natural opening in the rocks, soon to become known as the *"Golden Gate,"* and then to glide slowly into beautiful San Francisco bay.

He couldn't have arrived at a more exciting time. San Francisco had only been United States territory for about four years. The Americans had tried to buy it from Mexico a few years earlier, but then, when war broke out between the two countries, in 1846, the Americans took it by force.

GOLD!

The late 1840's saw the beginnings of the California gold rush. At first the town was deserted, men, women and children off to mother-lode country. Even the editor of the local newspaper, after writing a scathing attack on the residents of the town for getting caught up so easily in the mad rush to get rich quick, closed up shop, grabbed a shovel and a mule, and went racing after them.

Very soon, however, fortune hunters from all over the world crowded into the area. Abandoned ships choked the bay. Shacks and tents, mire and dust, fantastic prices, and a spate of gambling, drinking and vice broke out ashore.

An uncle of Dusty's had staked a few claims up in the gold fields, so, deserting the ship after his three month journey from Liverpool, the young lad from the Antrim coast went to help his uncle in the search for an 'easy,' fortune.

However, there was to be no fortune for Dusty in "them thar hills," and so he made his way to New York, secured a place on another ship, and came back to Liverpool.

Another trip took him aboard a whaling ship for two years, but he always made his way back to the Mersey and Liverpool.

Between sailing adventures he used to tramp the roads of England, going as far south as Land's End, in Cornwall.

ACTION ON THE BATTLEFIELD

Perhaps his greatest adventure was in 1867 when as a young man, still only twenty three, he enlisted in the Welsh Fusiliers. This took him to service in Malta and India and through the wildest part of the Khyber Pass in Afghanistan, where Lord Roberts was occupied in quelling some of the hill tribes who were in revolt.

Fifteen years he spent in the army and then came home, at last, to wander the less exciting roads and lanes of his homeland.

Eventually, his meanderings brought him to Coleraine, and the general area of Killowen. There, in later life, the young Speedy Moore would meet him and listen for hours to his tales of adventure and the sea.

Dusty Rhodes lived till he was ninety-five. When he became too old to wander the highways and byways of Ulster he went to live in Ballycastle.

As Speedy puts it, *"Quietly he crossed the vale of shadows on 21st April 1939."*

REMEMBERED AND HONOURED

But the story doesn't end there. On the 21st April 1990, the fiftieth anniversary of Dusty Rhodes' death, Speedy had the great honour of taking part in a ceremony to commemorate the poet's life.

At St. Patrick and St. Brigid's burying ground, Ballycastle, a select group of people, including members of the local Dusty Rhodes Appreciation Group, gathered to watch another local man, Seamus Clarke, unveil a tablet to the memory of the itinerant poet.

"Ah!, who can sing the song of the moor,
With its quickening and rushing wind;
Its curving breast and endless span
Of the hills and shadows find?"

THE LARGY POET

Another man whose skill with the pen influenced the young Moore was Samuel Connor, better known as "The Largy Ploughman Poet."

For years his poetry had helped fill the pages of the Northern Constitution and it was loved by the paper's large readership.

Speedy, and his sister Annie were firm devotees of the simple poet. They looked forward each week to hearing their mother read his latest contribution and very often, in these, Samuel Connor extolled his lovely Roe Valley.

"Hail fair scenes of matchless beauty,
Sweetest spot along the Roe;
Grandeur wild reigns round thine alleys
Where the sunlit waters glow.
Neath those summits famed in story
How the billows dance and play,
Laughing in their silvery glory,
Dashing up their churning spray."

FAREWELL TO THE ROE

Alas, like many another poor soul in this unfortunate country, Samuel Connor found it necessary to emigrate to foreign climes in search of a better life. With his wife and family of seven, he emigrated to Canada in 1925. How sad it must have been for them to leave behind friends, relatives and their native soil.

"Farewell, farewell, my native braes,
Where I have spent sweet childhood days,
I now must sing my parting strain
To scenes I ne'er may see again.
'Tis not without a bitter sigh,
That I break friendship's golden tie;
To foreign scenes fate bids me go
Adieu, ye bonnie banks of Roe."

Samuel Connor and his family settled in Brampton, Ontario, in those days a quiet little village on the outskirts of Toronto. They prospered, and to the delight of many in the North West of Ulster, Samuel continued to send poetic compositions for publication in the local papers. He set down his pen for the last time on 2nd October 1958 and was mourned by all who knew him.

Thankfully, in 1990, a book of Samuel Connor's poems was published. Entitled *"The Vale of the Roe,"* it was compiled by Conly George. Speedy Moore had the great joy of writing the foreword for it.

THE BUTTERMILK MAN

Of all the characters Speedy Moore came into contact with in his boyhood days around old Killowen, Mick, the buttermilk man, was his favourite.

There were plenty of such rounds men back in those days. They came on set days each week, their low dray carts pulled by a small horse or a pony, and loaded with that thick sour buttermilk that you never see nowadays.

Buttermilk is what's left over after full cream milk has been churned and the butter taken off it. However, modern methods of manufacture have enabled creameries to extract a lot more from the original milk, so there's a lot less left in the final buttermilk. Very few people would venture to drink today's buttermilk, but back in Speedy's childhood days it was a popular thirst quencher. It went well, too, with a couple of good big floury spuds and a dollop of country butter. It's main use, though, was for baking soda bread, a delicacy which graced every Ulster table in those days, and one of the king pins of the famous Ulster fry.

A HERO

Mick, the buttermilk man who became a kind of a hero to Speedy, was a bent-over little man with an enormous moustache. This hairy growth partly concealed the bowl of a clay pipe which seemed to be as a much a part of Mick as any other feature of his anatomy.

He stuffed the pipe with a strong tobacco and smoked it constantly, spitting every so often, and sending the brown, watery stream an endless distance.

Speedy became quite friendly with Mick and used to accompany him on his rounds. He did this for two years and during all that time he never knew Mick to wear anything but the same garments. 'Garments,' is hardly the word for the clothes that hung on his back. They were patched beyond recognition. As time went on more and more patches, of different colours, were added until hardly any of the original material could be seen.

On Tuesdays and Saturdays Speedy was ready when Mick arrived on the cart, loaded up with buttermilk and a few bags of turf, and pulled by his old roan mare 'Jill.'

Speedy hopped aboard, his bare legs hanging down between the cart shafts and, as soon as he was settled, Mick handed him the reins. What a proud moment for the wee lad.

"If you were to put me behind the wheel of a Rolls Royce today, it wouldn't compare with the joy I experienced as captain of old Mick's horse and cart," says Speedy.

Mick and his colleagues were partial to a drop of strong drink, from time to time, and used to frequent a particular bar in old Killowen. After an hour or so, when the drink had time to work, Mick would tend to become a bit opstreperous. Believe it or not, business rivalry between buttermilk men could be tough. When the drink was in, it added to the flames of competition and soon the pub was alive with shouting and yelling and bad language.

Despite Mick being small of stature and the very antithesis of the body builder, he was quick to put up the fists and would have squared up to Jack Dempsey at times like these.

However, the fighting spirit was knocked out of them all in a moment when the proprietor of the bar, a very strict man and anxious to hold on to his licence, called *"Time please,"* at the stroke of ten o'clock. The rowdy clientele, as one man, obediently set down their glasses and filed out into the street - then marched round the gable end of the tavern and in through the ever open back door.

SECRET MEDICINE

Mick carried four large cans on his cart and now and again there'd be one smaller can in between these bigger ones. Once, when Mick's back was turned, Speedy plucked up the courage to look inside this smaller can. He discovered that it contained an unusual sparkling white liquid, much thinner than the buttermilk. He ventured to ask Mick what kind of a cow produced this strange liquid.

"Tis a tin cow," was Mick's abrupt answer. Then he added, just as abruptly *"Now keep your mouth shut and mind your own business, or I'll be getting myself another man!"*

Suitably chastened, Speedy decided not to say another word about the wee can and to ask no more questions. But he couldn't help giving it a lot of thought.

His curiosity was even more heightened when, one day, his rounds with Mick took him down to Coleraine dockside.

At the sound of a docker's clear, sharp whistle Jill, the mare stopped dead in her tracks.

The dockers', faces black and sweaty from heaving coal and timber, gathered round Mick's cart in eager anticipation. Each held a tin mug in his hand and, one by one, Mick filled them with the thin white liquid from the wee can.

As they downed the precious draft and expelled great sighs of satisfaction their eyes brightened and their tempers improved. Speedy never tells us exactly what was in this wee can, that's if he ever knew, but whatever it was, it was powerful stuff. Like myself, though, I'm sure you can hazard a fairly accurate guess!

A SAD END

One Tuesday afternoon Speedy waited for Mick and Jill, as usual. However, the hours passed and the devoted partnership never arrived. He waited till it was almost dusk and then, with a heavy heart and dragging feet, made his way slowly home.

The weeks rolled into months, but there was never any sign of the little buttermilk man and his trusty mare. Speedy resigned himself to the fact that he would never see them again.

However, providence, or fate some would call it, works in unusual ways. In his boyhood days Speedy had a sweet and tuneful voice. Accompanied by a mandolin he had borrowed, he would croon a few of the popular ballads of the time.

His talent was in demand at parties and social gatherings and, on one memorable Christmas, he was invited to entertain the inmates of the local workhouse.

As Speedy strummed his mandolin and sang to the unfortunate creatures gathered before him, his eyes wandered over the crowd.

What a pathetic and sorry sight. The men were dressed in baggy suits of heavy black material and their hair was cut closely to the scalp. The women and girls wore striped uniforms, thick black stockings and nailed boots that Speedy thought would have been better fitted to ploughmen.

Suddenly, Speedy spotted a familiar face. It was Mick the buttermilk man. When his act was finished Speedy dashed down to embrace his old friend. He listened to his woeful tale. Jill had succumbed to the bullet from a vet's gun after breaking a foreleg. Without her, Mick, who had lived alone, was lost.

After that Speedy called to see him regularly. He took him a little tobacco for his old clay pipe, and sat and listened to his stories from former days.

Then, one day, he was gone. A workhouse official directed Speedy to Mick's last resting place, a cemetery on the Ballycastle Road.

Speedy stood looking down on the unmarked grave. There wasn't even a flower on it. All around it were rows of paupers' mounds covered with grass and weeds. Tears filled his eyes as he exclaimed *"Oh God, what a horrible place to bury a hero."*

Chapter Four

THE MAD BARBER

Arthur Letson ran the barber's shop, in old Killowen, and was a character in his own right. Other characters from the area often called into his shop, whether or not they needed a haircut, and were always welcome. Arthur enjoyed their company and the crack and sometimes, when the arguments became heated or rowdy, he found himself compering debates as well as coifing heads.

As well as being a master wit, Arthur was a kind of unofficial local councillor. Almost everyone in the street, indeed the district, came to him with their problems. Very sincerely, Arthur would do his best to advise, encourage and help. But he was not to be fooled.

On one occasion, a local crafty individual tried it but discovered that Arthur wasn't as easy a mark as he imagined.

SUICIDAL TENDENCIES

This particular individual had the habit of periodically going on the booze. At these times he suddenly acquired suicidal tendencies and succeeded in extracting money from soft-hearted people with the story that he was fed up with life and that his only options were either the river or a spoonful of arsenic.

The 'softies' invariably fell for this tale, dipped their hand in a pocket, and gave the crafty rascal a few shillings to go and have a strong drink and forget about poison, the river and troubles.

With a confidence that grows with success the scrounger approached Arthur Letson, the barber, knowing him to have a kind heart.

"Sir," he said in a shaky tone, *"I just can't stand this cruel world another day .. would you be kind enough to lend me a razor .. a good sharp one?"*

Without a word of reply, Arthur picked up a razor, gave it a couple of quick rubs on the leather strop, and handed it to the schemer with the admonition, *"Make sure you put it in your will that the razor is my property."*

In two seconds the scrounger was gone - and without the razor.

BIRDS AND FISH

Arthur Letson was a keen cage-bird fancier and a first class angler. Among his collection of canaries were a number of Irish singing birds which it was quite legal to keep in captivity back in those days.

Just after the end of the first World War Arthur was fishing at the famous Dugan's Bay, on the Bann estuary; a great spot for sea-trout. As was the custom then, before the advent of long rubber waders, the men removed their trousers, their long-johns and fastened the front and the tail of their shirts together. The fastening was done with a big safety pin, similar to the way a baby's nappy is held together. This meant they could wade out into the deep water without the extremities of the shirt floating on the surface.

The removing of men's trousers in public would have caused uproar in those far off more prudent days.

Dugan's Bay, however, was well off the beaten track and the possibility of ladies passing by and being offended by sights they weren't accustomed too, was minimal.

With his shirt tails duly pinned, Arthur was well out into the deep, casting a tempting fly over the deep waters that gently flowed about him. He was a superb angler and in his hands a fishing rod looked as light as a fairy wand.

As happens at times likes this, the repetitive action of casting the line, most times unsuccessfully, becomes almost automatic. Arthur's mind began to wander as he looked about him, enjoying the beauty of the countryside. Suddenly, he spotted a young cock lark on the bank. It was just what he needed for his cage bird collection and quickly he decided it should be his.

THE CHASE

He waded ashore, laid down his rod and sped off on the trail of the bird. The lark could only fly a few yards at a time and this served to encourage, tempt even, Arthur to keep on its trail.

He zigzagged this way and that, determined to lay his hands on this feathered prize. At times he jumped into the air. At others he scurried along close to the ground, like a bloodhound. But try as he might, the lark eluded him.

Just as Arthur was at the height of this frenzied chase, two other anglers came down the estuary in a boat. Blacksmith, Bob McDowell and postman, Paddy Cunning were out for a quiet afternoon to try their luck at the trout too.

Neither Paddy nor Bob could see the small lark, but Letson's mad dance was clearly evident.

Resting on his oars for a moment, Paddy Cunning shouted to Bob, *"Will you take a look at this. Yon fellow with the bare legs has gone cuckoo. What's he dancing round them hills for."*

HE'S MAD

Old Bob reeled in his line and looked in the direction of Paddy's pointing finger. When his eyes fixed on the spot his mouth dropped open, the pipe fell out of his it and he exclaimed, *"By heavens you're not far wrong Paddy. He's mad!"*

In a moment he had delved into the depths of his fishing bag and produced a pair of binoculars. However, by the time he fumbled them out of their case, propped them on his nose and got them into focus, the lark had disappeared and Arthur had given up the chase.

"It's that fellow Letson from Killowen," he called to Paddy. *"He's not long back from the war, poor soul. Maybe that's what's put him round the bend."* Then returning to his fishing he added *"For his own good I'll report his mad dance to the proper authorities tomorrow. It's better to get insanity stopped before it goes too far!"*

A couple of mornings later, a dispensary doctor, Creery by name, came to see the mad dancer. The doctor was a serious looking official but, as kindly as he could, he explained the reason for his visit. Arthur looked at him ior a moment and then, with a wry smile, explained the chase after the elusive lark.

There's no record of how the doctor reacted to Arthur's confession of his own 'larking' about, but the shame that the two 'ship borne' observers experienced is well documented. They felt a right pair of 'eejits,' but in the end they joined in a hearty laugh over the affair.

THE LANDED GENTRY

Two childhood experiences illustrate the extremes of kindness and cruelty of the times Speedy Moore grew up in.

One afternoon he was making his way back to school after the lunch time fishing trip. Just before he got to the school gates he was met by a pony and trap. The trap was driven by a gentleman and beside him sat a lady passenger. Speedy stopped by the roadside to allow them to pass. As the pony came alongside it spied the boy with the fishing rod over his shoulder. In retrospect, perhaps it thought this was another of these cruel humans with a whip - but we'll come to that.

The pony shied, raised its forelegs in the air and pranced about for a bit. It quickly settled, however, and young Speedy made his way onwards to school.

Just as he was about to step through the gates he heard a shout from behind. Wheeling round in surprise he found himself standing face to face with the driver of the pony and trap.

The man was in a state of intoxication, his bloodshot eyes conveyed his anger, and the whip he brandished confirmed his intentions towards the child before him.

DEFENCELESS

As he raised the whip and brought it down with all his strength Speedy became hysterical.

The first blow brought him to the ground. Once in that defenceless state the cruel bully had no difficulty in whipping him incessantly around his bare legs and body. Mercifully, he lost consciousness.

When the school principal arrived on the scene the gentleman gave his reasons for the whipping. He accused Speedy of frightening his young blood pony and expressed no sense of sorrow for what he had done to the child.

It is just possible that the pony was frightened by the boy standing by the roadside holding something that, to it, looked like a whip. On the other hand it might not have been frightened by Speedy, at all. In any event, it didn't warrant the attack that had been launched against him.

Speedy was taken home and when his thin jersey was removed, a mass of ugly purple scars, some of them oozing blood, was revealed. When his mother saw the mess her only son was in she broke down and wept for hours. As if she hadn't suffered enough.

Next day Speedy's mother stayed off work to report the matter to the police. However, her time was wasted.

The police would only answer, *"Your boy might have caused a nasty accident ... he deserved the whipping."*

Such was the sympathy for a poor, widow mother in those far off times.

TWO LAWS

Visits to every solicitor in town met the same response. *"You would only be putting your head against a stone wall taking a case against a man of such stature in the community. Away home woman and forget about it."*

And there was the crux of the problem. The man who had subjected a child on his way to school to such a merciless beating was no ordinary man. He was a titled gentleman, the owner of a large estate and of great influence in the area.

The situation that prevailed in those days was best summed up by a clergyman who called to give comfort to Speedy and his mother. *"It's a sad fact but a true one,"* he said. *"But in this country there's one law for the rich and another one for the poor."*

THE MILK OF HUMAN KINDNESS

The imposing Manor House was the home of the Right Hon. Hugh T. Barrie, D.L., M.P., and his kindly wife. The house stood in spacious grounds overlooking the river Bann, on the Killowen side of the borough.

Speedy's aunt, Mary Jane Moore, was a knitting companion of Mrs. Barrie and used to visit the big house regularly.

Sometimes when a function was being held, or during spring cleaning, Speedy's mother would be asked to give a hand. To keep Speedy out of mischief he was taken along too, and allowed to run, more or less, freely in the grounds. The young lad, raised in the streets of the town, was suddenly given a great new sense of freedom.

What adventures were played out among the trees and bushes of that country estate! Battles were fought and won! Fair princesses were rescued from the clutches of evil kings! New lands were discovered and charted. It was a whole new world to the young lad and he enjoyed every moment of it.

On one sharp December day Speedy stood watching the gardeners at work. Mrs Barrie looked out of the window and saw him shivering in the winter air. She called to her friend, Mary Jane, pointed out the state the child was in, and asked if she thought his mother would be offended if she offered him a coat.

No objections were expressed and very quickly Speedy was called inside. At first he thought he was in for a rebuke for some misdemeanour but, as Mrs Barrie steered him towards the spacious drawing room, his fears were allayed.

THE COAT

In front of the big, heartsome log fire, which burned the full length of the hearth, he stood answering Mrs Barrie's questions In the background his aunt, Mary Jane, anxious that his behaviour before this auspicious lady wouldn't let the family down, sent out all types of hand signals to him. At last Mrs Barrie motioned him to have a seat.

"Would you like coffee," she asked.

Speedy nodded, although he'd never tasted coffee in his life. Mrs Barrie gave some instruction to one of her maids and went upstairs for the coat. While she was gone aunt Mary Jane didn't let the time pass uselessly. She proceeded to give young Speedy a lecture on good manners, behaviour in the presence of a lady, and how to become a gentleman.

At last, thankfully, Mrs Barrie returned with the coat. It was made of soft moleskin and had a purple velvet collar and sturdy brown buttons. The good lady fitted it on and Aunt Mary Jane's nimble fingers did up the buttons.

A gentle chorus of 'ooohs' and 'aaahs' rang around the room. On hearing a whisper from the parlour maid, the kitchen and domestic staffs had sneaked in for a peep at this sight, and had brought Speedy's mother with them.

Everyone was in general agreement that the coat was a perfect fit; that it looked well; and that it would last many a day.

The latter statement was much more true than anyone there expected. When Speedy grew out of the coat it was passed on to another boy. He, in turn, gave it to someone else. Speedy claims that, in his youth and manhood, he frequently saw the coat rendering great service.

And he reports that, another former custodian of the coat, George Loughrey, champion boxer, now maker of champions, claims to have seen *"the coat,"* giving faithful service in recent years, in the Garvagh area.

An interesting footnote to this story is that, the original wearer and owner of the coat was Walter Barrie. In later years he rose to the position of Chairman of Lloyds and was knighted for his services to the financial world. Perhaps it's fitting that the lad who once wore his handed down coat, had the task of writing his obituary in 1990.

Chapter Five

LIFE'S FAVOURITE PASTIME

Angling and piscatorial pursuits have been a passion with Speedy Moore, for as long as he can remember. Those forays to that sheugh in Cameron's Marsh, as a schoolboy, served only to whet his appetite for greater shores.

In this he was fortunate. Two local anglers, Sam Gough and John Millar were the first to take him over the Coleraine mountain to witness the sights and delights of the Roe Valley, with its very own famous salmon river.

On a pleasant Saturday afternoon in July the two men and the boy set off in John Millar's open car. Sam Gough sat beside him in the front and, although there was a small windscreen, they both wore goggles. Speedy sat on the raised dickey seat behind them enjoying the grand view as they trundled along.

MILLAR'S MOTOR CAR

It was Speedy's first journey in a motor car and he was thrilled with the prospect of this new experience. Not many boys of ten were introduced to the thrills of motoring back then. They chugged along at a steady pace, perhaps twenty-five miles an hour; slow by today's standards but faster than any milk-float or buggy he had ever sat on.

For the first time he felt the rush of the wind blowing through his hair and lapped up the exhilaration of *'speed'* on four wheels. As the engine purred its merry tune Speedy drunk in the wonders of the sights about him.

The countryside had on its best cloak of summer green. The purple clad mountains rose majestically before them and, here and there a mountain stream gurgled its way towards the Lough, and the sea.

In those far off days the pace of life was much slower and yet the enjoyment of life, much greater. The journey from Coleraine to the river Roe, where they were to fish, must have taken at least three quarters of an hour. Fishing time is precious time, yet John Millar had no hesitation in stopping the car at the highest point on the road so they could feast their eyes on the breathtaking spectacle of Lough Foyle stretching away below them. Its sparkling waters mirrored the beautiful canopy of the blue sky and lapped gently on the quiet shores of Donegal, miles away.

BREAKNECK SPEED

Setting off, down the other side, John put the foot down. The little car went faster and faster until it reached the incredible speed of forty miles an hour! It may have gone even faster but Sam, whether cautious or just plain scared, appealed to John to employ discretion and apply the brakes, for the sake of their three necks. They arrived - and returned - quite safely.

Over the years Speedy enjoyed many return trips to the Roe with John Millar and Sam Gough. At first his time was spent helping the two men, carrying their food baskets, assisting them with simple tasks, gaffing the odd fish. He used to watch, with amazement, their skill as they handled those 18 foot long, lance-wood fly rods. They made it all look so easy and he wondered if, someday, he would demonstrate such skill himself. He often wondered, too, if he'd ever own such fine fishing tackle as they did.

Those visits to the Roe brought him into contact with many angling characters. Doctors, solicitors, business men and factory workers; all feel the call of the riverside, and all are brought together by this most popular of sports.

TALKING TO THE FISH

Bob McCallion, a local blacksmith, stands out above many of the others in Speedy's memory. He was an expert fly caster and when he hooked a salmon he displayed an interesting characteristic. He spoke to the fish as if it were a pet dog.

"Come on now my wee darlin' and stop your nonsense."

"Go on girl, give yourself a good run for the last time, for you're going to join Uncle Bob on the bank this fine summer's day."

"That's a good girl. Now don't get too rough, two can play at that game you know. No resting now, I can't spend all day here."

But if he happened to loose the fish, his affectionate patter quickly dried up.

He would stamp on the river bank in disgust and shout *"You oul' rascal, you're only an oul' spoil-sport."*

A STRANGE CATCH

As well as being a first class angler Bob MCallion was also a great story teller. Many a time he entertained the rest of the lads over a glass in the local hostelry. The corner of his mouth twitched in a devilish smile as he began one of his favourite tales.

"An oul' witch used to live on the other side of the Roe, not far from here. Dear help the unfortunate angler she found trespassing on her bit of land. This oul' biddy also kept about a hundred ducks which, to anglers, were a continual pollution, splashing and spoiling the fishing pools.

"One morning I accidentally lassoed the oul' doll's pride and joy - a big drake. I'm telling you it fairly made the reel scream. You'd have thought I'd hooked a fresh-run, ten pound cock salmon. The commotion attracted the oul' witch and she and her two dogs came running down the field.

"She stood watching this melee for a couple of minutes and then shouted at me "That's my drake you're sporting sir!" Well, as the wide river divided us, I politely informed her that it would soon be my drake, if the line didn't give way. It turned out to be a pleasant change from the monotony of salmon steaks." Bob concluded his story with a chuckle.

Years later Speedy bumped into the old blacksmith again.

He was standing at the Limavady Bridge, looking forlornly at the water below him. His fishing tackle had long since been laid aside; all he was left with were memories.

Speedy thought of a verse he had learned years before.

*"My sledge and hammer have declined.
My bellows pipe has lost its wind;
My forge is gone, my fire's decayed,
And in the dust my vise is laid.
My coal is spent, my iron is gone,
My nails are drove, my work is done!"*

INFLUENCES

Speedy's young life was continually being influenced and moulded by characters like these.

Another was Sam Henry, who taught Bible class on Sunday afternoons at the second Coleraine company of the Boys Brigade.

Sam was a gifted, cultured man and he held his pupils spellbound as he brought to life the great stories from the Bible.

A native of Coleraine, he was a leading authority on Irish folk-lore and natural history. He was a keen student of Ulster genealogy and archaeology, which he broadcast, lectured and wrote about regularly.

Sam was the author of nine books and frequently contributed racily written articles to the local newspapers and to journals farther afield. He had a richly stored mind, a retentive memory, and a seemingly inexhaustible fund of humour and anecdote.

When the Boys Brigade company went camping to Ballycastle, Sam Henry went with them, as did young Speedy.

Sam was a great student of wildlife and, taking Speedy with him, he would stroll down to the banks of the river Margy to observe nature, first hand. They would watch the swallows dive and weave in the stillness of the evening air, gobbling up the freshly hatched young flies that hovered above the placid stream. Or they would follow the path of a sleek Otter as it scurried along the river bank and then plunged into the dark waters in search of supper.

"THE OUL' LAMMAS FAIR."

After a while Sam would pick up his violin, draw the bow across the strings a few times, to check the tuning and then launch into a verse or two of *"If I were a blackbird,"* or *"The oul' Lammas fair."*

Changing the mood from time to time, Sam picked up his tin whistle and rattled out a few Irish jigs and reels.

Sam Henry could rightly claim to be the man who gave *"The Oul' Lammas Fair,"* it's world popularity.

The song was written by a Ballycastle woodcarver, John McAuley. Sam Henry heard him sing the song, noted down the words and music and gave them their baptism.

THE JARVEY

By profession, Sam was a customs and excise officer and, in that capacity, relied a lot on jarveys and their jaunting cars. Jarveys were looked upon as local encyclopaedias, expected to know where everyone lived and how to locate every winding road and farm lane.

One night Sam Henry was detained in the town of Garvagh, long after lighting up time. Being a Government official he was a bit concerned about this but entrusted himself to the care of Pat Hackett, the jarvey.

They hadn't travelled very far when a stern voice called out in the dark *"Halt!"*

Sam whispered to Pat the jarvey *"I doubt we're in for it now."*

Pat whispered back *"It'll be all right,"* and then shouted out *"Is that you constable?"*

Back came the answer *"Is that you Pat?"*

"Aye, indeed it's me. It's a wild dark night, isn't it?"

"It is that," agreed the constable, adding *"Well goodnight, and safe home."*

Pat whipped up the horse and away they went, towards Coleraine. Nothing was said till they were safely clear of the town, then Sam leaned over and nudged the jarvey. *"That was a near thing Pat. How did we get away with it?"*

"Awe, that's easy," replied Pat. *"He's courtin' my sister."*

SINISTER TRANSPORT

That same jarvey, Pat Hackett, owned a hearse which he hired out to overworked undertakers. He drove the rig himself.

On a dark, wet winters night, driving the empty hearse from Ringsend to Coleraine, he pulled up to give a lift to a stranger, walking alone.

The lone stranger was rather taken aback when he realised what type of vehicle he was being offered a ride in. In those days, in rural Ireland there was no more sinister mode of transport for a living man than a hearse.

Pat, the jarvey-cum-hearse driver, suggested his passenger would be much more comfortable, certainly drier, inside the hearse. Taking his courage in his hands, the stranger scrambled inside the coffin compartment of the hearse, remembering Pat's admonition to keep his head near the air hole.

A little further down the road the hearse pulled to a standstill again to give a lift to a second stranger. There being room for only one body inside the hearse, this second man was invited up on to the seat beside the driver.

THE GREAT ESCAPE

As they rattled along in the wet and darkness the second man turned to Pat and enquired,

"Are you never feared in the dark in this thing?"

"Not at all," said Pat. *"I never give it a thought."*

The a voice from within cried: *"Maybe if you were in here you'd be feared!"*

The passenger on the driver's seat left as if he'd been propelled from a gun. He was never heard of again. One supposes he eventually got a second ride in a hearse. There'd be no getting away on that occasion.

Chapter Six

FRESH PASTURES

At the age of eleven Speedy said good-bye to the old Killowen National School and crossed the Bann each morning to attend the Hon. the Irish Society's Boys School. His mother hoped that, at last, her son would take a keener interest in learning and make something of himself. Perhaps he would become a doctor or a lawyer, and be in a position to serve the community and make a good living.

Going to a new school, with a fancy sounding name, however, made no difference to Speedy Moore. He was not a keen academic and was, it seemed, unlikely ever to be so.

That didn't mean that his time at secondary school was altogether wasted. Far from it! There were new faces at the new school, new people to meet, new friends to make. Speedy made the best of the opportunities, some so outstanding and memorable that they've left an impact to this day.

BIG HARRY

Thomas Henry Turbitt didn't realise what an impact the kindly act of sharing his lunch one day with two boys from poor homes would make. One of them, a lad called Moore, would remember his deed of kindness and write about it in his newspaper column years later.

It was this same teacher, affectionately referred to as "Big Harry," who encouraged Speedy to join the Boys' Brigade. And it was through the Boys' Brigade that Speedy met that other wonderful character, already referred to, Sam Henry.

Another teacher, who shall remain anonymous, didn't realise that as he abused his authority to administer corporal punishment, namely the cane, he was inscribing an indelible mark on the heart and soul of his pupil, again young Moore.

The master had already raised welts on Speedy's left hand. As he asked for the second hand to be held out for a whacking, Speedy squared up to him and he rushed from the room in hysterics.

EXPELLED!

He returned with the principal, who was quick to inform the defiant student that there was no place in his school for boys who tried to bully the master. He omitted to mention that there seemed to be plenty of room for bullying teachers. Speedy was summarily expelled from the school.

Thankfully, before news of this disgrace reached his mother's ears, a local businessman used his influence to get Speedy reinstated. His actions weren't forgotten either.

It was through attending the Hon. Irish Society's School that Speedy met John 'Gunner' McGonigle. Gunner was a pupil at St. Malachy's School and the thing that made him attractive to Speedy was that he had a morning job at Peter Morelli's ice-cream factory.

Gunner managed to get Speedy into Morelli's as his assistant. The situation was vacant because the previous occupant of the job, the gluttonous 'Touser' Simpson, had been sacked by Mrs Morelli, for testing the ice-cream too often during production.

LOVELY, LOVELY ICE-CREAM!

Speedy and Gunner worked in the freezer house, where the ice-cream was made under Peter Morelli's strict eye. They started at a quarter to six in the morning and worked through till about ten to nine, taking turns to crank the heavy handle that mixed the ice-cream in large vats. The ingredients were mixed to a secret recipe, hidden in Peter's heart. Neither

Speedy or Gunner were allowed to know it.

Peter Morelli was born in Casalattico, Italy, in 1885. Like his father and brothers, he became a professional glass-blower. Another member of the family, Peter's Uncle Joe, came to Coleraine around the turn of the century, bringing the family recipe with him. Joe Morelli opened an ice-cream parlour at Bridge Street, Coleraine, in 1900, just four days before the Bann regatta. It is reported that he did a roaring trade. If you've ever tasted Morelli's ice-cream, you'll know why.

Eventually young Joe Morelli came to Coleraine and worked for a while in his uncle's shop. His winning ways made him immediately acceptable to the Coleraine people and he settled in very well.

Indeed, when uncle Joe decided to quit the borough, young Peter stayed on, got his own freezer and hand cart, and did quite a good trade in the summer months. Ice cream is always popular in the triangle area.

ROMANCE

Joe was popular too, with a young local lass, Annie Diamond. They met in 1905 and a courtship began. Alas, however, there were frequent partings for the young pair. The winter storms send white foamed waves crashing on the beaches of the North Atlantic coast and the sea breezes are whipped up to gale force. Tourists desert the place and the ice cream trade disappears. This drove Joe back to Italy every winter to take up the glass blowing trade again.

To Annie's delight he came 'home' for good in 1910 with a hard earned £40 in his pocket. With the money he established a business in Stone Row, Coleraine. The following year he married Annie Diamond and they settled down to a happy life together.

As well as the parlour-cum-cafe in Stone Row, they had a new pony and cart on the road so they could take their delicious ice-cream to distant places. But there was a lot less money about for such luxuries back in those poorer days and business wasn't all plain sailing.

Joe Morelli was disappointed and about to close up shop and go back to the only other thing he knew, glass blowing, when a remarkable thing happened. One day a good customer, Bob Love, was opening the door to come into the cafe for his morning cuppa when a little bird flew in past him and perched on the sill of an inside window.

"That's lucky," exclaimed Bob.

It was a simple, brief statement - a casual remark really - but the distressed Peter gave thought to it and after some reflection decided not to quit the ice-cream business after all.

The hundreds of thousands of people who, down through the years, have sat and supped the delightful creations served up in a Morelli ice-cream parlour, will be eternally grateful to that little bird which flew in and brought Peter and Annie Morelli such 'good luck.'

WORK

Speedy Moore, himself, had to demonstrate a fortitude akin to that of Peter Morelli in settling himself in steady employment.

He left school at fourteen and went to work in a small bicycle shop for the handsome sum of four shillings for a sixty-hour week. It was hardly a fortune, but he felt a proud fella' the first Friday night when he arrived home and planked his pay packet down on the table.

The bicycle shop job lasted for more than two years, during which time Speedy was growing all the while. Growing, not only in stature, but in self confidence too - boldness some would call it.

His mother's tempestuous scolding no longer held any fears for him, nor did it have any bearing on his young life. Speedy considered himself a man now. He was handing over a pay-packet on a Friday night. That meant, in his book, he could do as he liked for the rest of the week.

Doing as he liked, meant forgetting about church on Sundays and smoking in front of his mother and other people. The traces of discipline were now well and truly cast off, and Speedy Moore was setting out in search of all the fun and pleasure this world could offer him.

A HINT OF REBELLION

This firm, some might say, rebellious stand, saddened his mother greatly. But Speedy had made up his mind and, heartlessly, he brushed her appeals aside.

This new found boldness extended to his place of employment too. He was getting fed up with the bicycle-shop job and he and his boss weren't on the best of terms. Speedy thought that his two years' experience was worth another one and sixpence a week. The boss disagreed and offered him the half of it, nine pence. Humiliated, Speedy reached for his coat and said good-bye to bicycle fixing - at least as a means of earning a living.

Speedy claims that his next job is worthy of a place in the Guinness Book of Records. It lasted exactly eight minutes. If Speedy's account of what happened is accurate, it's a wonder it even lasted that long.

The job in the animal feed store involved carrying a two-hundred-weight bag of bran from the store to the lorry.

Two-hundred-weight in simple parlance is 228 lbs. That's over sixteen stones, or the weight of a six foot tall, well built man. Trouble is, a big, heavy man can hang on and so help himself to be carried. A big bag of bran can't do that - it has to be lifted bodily and also held onto. Speedy manfully tackled the task but went down under the weight, spilling three gallons of paint in the process.

The boss still had Speedy's employment cards in his hand. Dumfounded by the sight before him he handed the cards back and said *"Put yourself on a course of porridge and fresh eggs son, then come back to me."*

IN FATHER'S FOOTSTEPS

Depressed by this ignominious failure Speedy applied to the Railway Company, hoping to capitalise on his father's name and the fact that he had worked there for years.

In due course an invitation to come to railway headquarters, in Belfast, arrived. It was accompanied by a free travel voucher. This was to be Speedy's first visit to a big city. The prospect gripped him with excitement.

Arriving at headquarters, he was ushered into a large office, where two dignified gentlemen sat at a polished oak desk.

First he faced a barrage of questions. After this he was set down to do a difficult written test, which, through a tip off, he was well prepared for. The day's business was concluded with a stiff medical examination, tough enough, Speedy maintains, for soldiers going into battle.

There followed long anxious days of waiting for the postman to bring news of either success or failure.

Eventually, it came and conveyed great news. Speedy had passed all tests with flying colours and was to start work at Portrush Railway Station on Easter Monday, just three days away.

SUCCESS

There was unparalleled delight in the Moore house and, indeed, in the rest of the street. Speedy wept with joy as he hugged his mother. At last he had a job that would enable this hard working, sorely tried woman, to take life a little easier.

Aunt Mary Jane Moore and Aunt Annie Parkill, on hearing the good news made large contributions to what Speedy calls a "Family Circle," fund. This supplied the new, young railway executive with a fine suit, a shirt to match and, of course, a pair of smart shoes. A man must dress appropriately for his job! *"After all,"* they thought, *"we could be rigging out the future head of the railways in Ireland."*

Come Easter Monday morning Speedy was standing outside Portrush Railway Station half an hour before the expected time. His new suit fitted like a glove and out of the breast pocket there protruded a pen and three sharp pencils. This lad wasn't going to be caught out, ill prepared, if there was a lot of paper work to do.

On the stroke of nine o'clock a small, portly man walked into the main concourse of the railway station. He was the station master, splendidly dressed in the uniform and gold braid scoop-cap of that high office.

HEADY ASPIRATIONS

Speedy took one look at this small, but august figure and imagined himself wearing a uniform identical to his in a few years, if he kept his nose clean. He observed him for a moment then, straightening his tie, pulling down his shirt cuffs to reveal a pair of sparkling Woolworth's links, and puffing out his chest, he presented himself to the boss.

Not a word was spoken till the little man had handed Speedy a mop, a pail, a brush and a scrubber. Then, pointing to the gents toilets he growled: *"They're all yours, and make sure you clean the bogs and hand-wash basins properly."*

As Speedy entered the sickening stench of those hitherto neglected quarters, he reflected on the stringent tests he had undergone in Belfast a few weeks previously. *If this is what's required to qualify me for cleaning toilets, what would I need to be a humble ticket collector? A degree from Queen's University?"*

Chapter Seven

SUMMER IN THE 'PORT'

Speedy Moore, being the astute and quick witted character he is, soon found that he didn't have to spend all his time sloshing out toilets. Anyway, there's only so much you can do with toilet cubicles - once they're clean, they're clean.

Portrush railway station was a busy place in those days; passengers came and went in the thousands. The wealthier classes had houses in the 'port', and they came for the fresh bracing air and the sea breezes in the summer months. There were lots of guest houses too, and families who rented these places were coming and going from May to September.

Holiday makers always have lots of luggage, more than they can carry, and when a willing young fellow offers to help carry it, he's a welcome sight. The people arriving in Portrush were in a holiday mood too, that made them more than willing to part with a few bob, as a tip, to the nice young man who helped them. Speedy never spurned their generosity. In fact, in this way, he was able to supplement his thirty shillings a week railway pay, by a considerable amount.

Outside, in the spacious square, jarveys, with their ponies and traps, and taxi drivers waited to take the happy holiday makers to their summer destinations. Each platform porter had his favourite jarvey to whom he took his trade. Speedy's was George McMullan.

GEORGE MCMULLAN

George, a former jarvey, had sold his horse and jaunting car and invested in the latest form of transport, a Model T Ford. A man of some vision, he could see that the mechanical revolution was here to stay. During the summer he did a fairly good trade, but the money he earned had to last him through the lean winter months.

He was a controversial character, George McMullan, and manys the scrap he was a part of.

Once, in the days of the jaunting car, he was taking a party of tourists from Portstewart to Portrush. On the way he met another jarvey with whom he had a 'crow to pick.'

"Here Sir," hold these reins for five minutes till I give this fellow a bit of a chastising," said George to the nearest passenger.

Jumping down from the jaunting car the wee man stopped the rival yoke and hauled the driver from the seat, to the ground.

What a grandstand view the passengers in the two jaunting cars had of the melee that ensued. Some of them were shocked by what they saw and yelled for the warring jarveys to desist. Others were of the mind that this was all part of the special tourist attractions laid on for visitors, and enjoyed every moment of it.

TRIUMPH FROM TRAGEDY

Alas, the dynamic George was to meet with a serious road accident which disabled him for life. Amazingly, it also had the effect of transforming him and changing his boisterous way of living. In his own words he told Speedy:

"As I lay in a hospital bed, suffering agony, and almost in the throes of death, I was brought to my senses. I realised I had let my creator down badly. There and then I accepted Him and his precious Word."

George McMullan recovered from his injuries and entered public life as a local councillor. He rose to become Chairman of Portrush Council and a stalwart servant of the working class people, from which background he had come.

For many years he gave them his loyal service as a member of various public bodies. He served on the Old Age Pensions Board and the Court of

Referees, which decided a person's case when appeals were made against refusals of benefit by the Ministry of Labour. All agreed that, in those offices of trust, he was scrupulously fair and helpful. After all, he had known what it was to be poor himself.

George McMullan, jarvey, taxi-driver, man of the people, Chairman of Portrush Council, and Justice of the Peace, passed peacefully into his Master's presence, holding the Bible - the Book which had been his guide through the latter years of his life - close to his breast. But in those latter years he had left a mark on his community, and on those who were privileged to know him.

THE EIGHT WONDER!

Reflections on the Portrush area also bring to mind, with no little degree of nostalgia, the wonderful Causeway Tram.

It ran from outside Portrush Railway Station, all the way to the Giant's Causeway, and has often been referred to as **"The Eighth Wonder of the World!"** Almost as wonderful, in Speedy's eyes, was the young man who acted as conductor on this famous tram.

Sam Twaddle hailed from the nearby town of Bushmills. His family ancestors, from an honourable Scottish clan, had settled there some three hundred years earlier.

Sam was a winsome character and blessed with what has often be described as, 'the gift of the blarney.' This gift was put to good use on the Causeway tram route where, as well as collecting fares, he used to entertain the passengers with his informed and interesting talks on the sights along the route.

In his fascinating drawl he described the history of the passing scenes, and then excelled with a special commentary on the ruins of Dunluce Castle. However, the high point of his tour was the Giant's Causeway.

FINN MACCOOL

The Causeway spreads its basaltic formations of honeycomb rocks on a beautiful coastline and the sight has amazed old and young for centuries. A steady flow of visitors still come to sit in the 'giant's chair,' or to photograph the awesome giant's 'pipe organ.' The phenomenon has puzzled the minds of geologists too, and many theories about it have been published.

Conductor Twaddle, however, favoured the more romantic 'giant,' theory. During each tram trip he would mesmerise his passengers with an account of how the Giant's Causeway came to be there. Delving back into the mists of time, he told of how the Irish giant, Finn MacCool had a dispute with his Scottish counterpart Jock McTavish.

So great was the hatred between the two protagonists that Finn MacCool began building a road, across the narrow stretch of water between North Antrim and Kintyre, so that a fight could take place. The Giant's Causeway is the beginning of that road. Alas - it was never finished!

Sam Twaddle's storytelling was so accomplished that many of his passengers, alighting from the tram at the end of the line, continued on to inspect the Causeway, in the firm belief that a giant once really did reign there.

NEVER ON A SUNDAY!

Of course, the causeway tram had its critics, mainly because it ran seven days a week. Back in those days, the strict keeping of the Sabbath day was the norm, rather than the unique. A public vehicle that took fare paying passengers, on trips of sheer pleasure, on Sunday, was not popular with many people, especially the clerics.

The most outspoken of all against the Sunday tram was the Rev. Jonathan Simpson, the minister of Portrush Presbyterian Church.

One Sunday morning, whilst the good man was in the midst of public prayer, the train rattled its way round the corner near his church. Pausing for a moment the good man suspended his current line of thought and exclaimed:

"There you are Lord. I told you about the noise created by that awful thing on the Sabbath! Now you can see it, and hear it, for yourself."

Sadly, the Causeway Tram is no more. The rising popularity of the motor car, with its inherent convenience, drew passengers away from the old tram. Eventually, it was broken up and sold as scrap - a sad end for the world's first hydro-electric tramway.

One can only imagine what a lucrative tourist attraction it would be today.

ON YER BIKE!

The tips Speedy received for portering at Portrush Railway Station, enabled him to invest in something he'd had his eyes on for quite a while. The newly invented sports bicycles, with their lighter frames, turned down handle-bars, and sleek looks, had just come on the market. Speedy took a fancy to one of these machines and bought one, paying it up each week, on hire purchase.

He used it at first to cycle to and from work, saving the cost of the bus fares and, at the same time, increasing his own physical fitness.

Cycle races were also becoming popular and Speedy thought he could have a go at this sport, without disgracing himself. He took part in a number of races, in different parts of Counties Antim and Londonderry, and did quite well.

One of these races was to have an effect on him which would stay with him for the rest of his life.

Someone organised a sort of 'all-comers,' race, in the country. About forty competitors assembled, with one of the most motley collections of bicycles ever seen.

As well as eight stream-lined models, similar to Speedy's, there were vintage ladies and gents machines of all shapes and sizes.

There were no such things as special sports shorts or shirts, and crash helmets hadn't yet been heard of. Everyday clothes were the order, with scoop caps reversed to better cut through the summer breeze. Bicycle clips stopped the trouser legs from flapping in the wind, or getting wrapped up in the whirling chain.

A CIRCUS

The whole thing was like a circus, with men and boys pushing and clamouring for the best starting place.

For the organisers, it was a nightmare. They had never seen such a large entry.

The course was a four mile triangle along dusty, winding, country roads, and the competitors had to complete three laps of it, to make up the total distance of twelve miles. Three stewards officiated at the starting-point and two more observed the progress at the top hairpin bend.

At last the starter's flag dropped. With an untidy scramble, and lots of shouting from participants and spectators alike, the wonderfully assorted field of cycle-mounted hopefuls raced away.

Coming up to the hairpin bend, on the first lap, Speedy hung in behind the few lads who were ahead of him. They were punching into a strong breeze and he thought it a good idea to let those in front break its strength. When they rounded the hairpin, he would overtake the lot and set them a hot pace from there on.

However, just as he was about to take the sharp corner, his front tyre punctured. What a disappointment! Speedy's heart sunk in deep despair.

O WHAT A TANGLED WEAVE!

Surprisingly, the two stewards who were standing nearby, witnessed this predicament and were most sympathetic. They even helped Speedy to repair the puncture. With a word of gratitude, Speedy was about to re-join the race when one of the stewards suggested:

"The rest of the field will be here, on their second lap, in about three minutes. Just you stay hidden in the bushes till they've passed, then you can join in again, behind them.. You'll be back in the race!."

Speedy turned to the steward with a questioning gaze. The official continued:

"If necessary, we can always vouch for you; say that you did complete the first lap. Not a soul will be any the wiser."

"And would that convince the stewards at the starting point, if they've missed me," Speedy asked.

"Fiddlesticks," he retorted, *"It's a golden chance worth taking. Don't miss it."*

"Why are you doing this for me, a total stranger to you both?" Speedy enquired suspiciously.

"Well, if you win, you can split the prize money with Tom and me." He rubbed his hands gleefully and went on: *"Ten bob would get Tom and me a wheen of stout in oul' Biddy's this evening."*

YIELDING TO TEMPTATION!

Speedy thought of all the bother he'd gone to compete in the race. He had paid a half-crown entry fee and now ill luck, which had given him this puncture, had seen his hopes dashed. He thought, too, of the thrill it would be to cross the line ahead of all the others, and take the prize.

The carrot of temptation hung before him by these agents of evil was too much to resist. Since he had the assurance of their collusion, he thought it would be worth while taking a chance, stooping to roguery, and following their plan of deceit.

As Speedy nodded his approval of the plan, the crafty schemer rubbed his hands together again. Tom did the same.

Shortly, the still tightly bunched architects, now puffing and panting under the strain of their exertions, appeared at the hairpin bend. As soon as they had passed, Speedy emerged from his hiding place in the bushes and set off in hot pursuit.

Soon he was in the midst of his opponents and none of them seemed to notice that he'd been missing for a lap. Their puffs and groans encouraged Speedy. He reckoned a few of them wouldn't be there at the final flag.

Passing the starting point, Speedy kept as low as possible. He wanted to make sure of not drawing too much attention to himself. Once out of sight of the starting post, though, he pressed ahead, easing his way to the front. Not too quickly though, less his abundant energy should arouse suspicion. As he rounded the hairpin bend for the last time, the two crooked stewards gave him a hearty cheer. They could see the pints lined up on Biddy's bar.

Eventually, Speedy won the race with comparative ease. Obviously no-one noticed the missing lap; no-one said a word; and there was no stewards enquiry. Inside Speedy, however, there was an awful feeling of guilt. The crooked steward was assigned the job of handing out the prizes and as he presented Speedy with his envelope he called out to the crowd:

"Three cheers for this speedy merchant!"

Feeling jittery, lest someone should challenge his win, Speedy grabbed the envelope, stuffed it into his pocket, and high-tailed it back home as quick as he could. He didn't even wait to split the winnings with his crooked co-conspirators.

Reaching home, he ripped open the envelope to find it contained only five shillings, half the amount of the first prize. His partners in crime had taken their share and there wasn't a thing Speedy could do about it. A bargain had been struck and Speedy was learning the truth of the axiom - **pay day, some day!**

A NEW NAME

The next day he met Jack 'Bud' Fisher, a great footballer of the twenties, and a natural humorist. Jack addressed our hero as "Speedy," and the name stuck. He's been 'Speedy' Moore ever since.

He still regrets, though, the way he earned the name and hopes that readers will look upon his escapade, all those years ago, as more of boy-hood prank than a pre-meditated plan to deceive and defraud.

Chapter Eight

HIGHER AMBITIONS

When the great summer holiday season finished, at Portrush, Speedy's job finished with it. He was, more or less, written off the roll of employees.

Strangely, he didn't seem to mind for he couldn't see any future in scrubbing toilets. He had his sights on something much more ambitious.

Hoover was a fairly new name in those days and the company had just brought its amazing new carpet cleaning machine onto the market. Hoover was looking for salesmen and Speedy accepted a job with them. The company sent him to Dublin on a special training course.

Dublin was a long way from home and, very soon, the young lad from Coleraine was desperately home-sick.

DUBLIN'S FAIR CITY

Even then, Dublin was a big, bustling city with wide streets, massive public buildings, spacious parks, and miles and miles of built up areas. The young lad from the country felt lost in this concrete wilderness.

Time, however, is a great healer, and as Speedy slowly ploughed his way through his salesmanship course, he settled into this new environment. The sights already mentioned began to lay claim to his attention and what was even better, he made new friends.

THE LURE OF GOLD!

He returned to Coleraine with an evangelical enthusiasm for the product he was to sell. The borough council was changing from gas to electricity and, already, Speedy could see a fortune piling up. It looked like he had found his true vocation at last.

Professor Sam Fleming and his wife Bridget, lived in a long, single storey, thatched cottage in the middle of Coleraine. Speedy was very friendly with them and knew that theirs was one of the few houses in the street to have the luxury of carpeted floors. He also knew that they were extremely house proud. They were, he thought, ideal prospective customers.

Wide eyed, the genial couple listened to Speedy's glib line of patter. The weeks in Dublin's fair city had not been wasted. The professor and his wife readily agreed to allow a demonstration of this wonderful new contraption, in their home, the next day.

Speedy thought it would a wonderful opportunity to display this marvellous labour saving device to a wider audience, so he invited a number of housewives along to witness the demonstration. When they saw it beating, and sweeping, and cleaning, they would be easily convinced to part with their, or their husband's, hard earned cash.

The women came, every one of them, and they brought their friends too. Speedy had a large gallery of observers. He was overwhelmed with the enthusiastic response. However, much too clever to let it show, he concealed his excitement and went about the demonstration with vigour.

AN EPIC EVENT

After a homely address on the qualities of this new labour-saving device he laid the preparation for the practical part of the show. He opened three bags of white powder and spread their contents the full length and breadth of the carpet. He sprinkled the powder over the three piece suit, the walls, the curtains and anywhere else he thought it might have dramatic effect. Not content with this, he borrowed a shovel and added some real dirt form the street. This was going to be an impressive demonstration!

When everything was ready, he turned to the professor and enquired, *"Where's your socket, sir?"*

"My what?" the professor asked, obviously confused.

"Your electric socket, to plug the cleaner into?" explained Speedy.

"Oh!" he gasped, *"We don't have electric ... we only have gas."*

Well, you can imagine Speedy's confusion. He could feel his face burning red with embarrassment, and at the same time he was sick to the pit of his stomach. What a predicament ... and this his first demonstration.

HUMILIATION AND EMBARRASSMENT!

However, the professor's house couldn't be left in that state. It had to be returned to it's former pristine condition. Speedy had to go and scrounge the use of a long length of electric flex, to bring the power to the mess. The gallery of housewives remained to witness what they considered to be a domestic miracle. The day was saved and Speedy could look the professor and his wife straight in the face again.

Speedy still feels sore about that incident for, in his opinion, it should never have happened. You see, Hoover salesmen were supplied with a list of people who had electricity installed in their homes. This list was provided by the Northern Ireland Electricity Board and one of the names on it was that of Samuel Fleming, Killowen Street, Coleraine. Speedy's embarrassment and inconvenience was caused, he feels, by bungling officialdom.

THE PROFESSOR!

The aforementioned professor Sam Fleming and his wife Bridget, ran a small store in old Killowen. It stocked everything from the proverbial needle to an anchor. It was also one of the first places in the area to offer 'tick.'

The couple's many customers were each issued with their own tick-book. Goods purchased during the week were marked down in the book, then, at the end of the week, or when times were better, the debts were paid off.

The professor, himself, wasn't all that keen on this form of making a living. He had show business in his veins and would far rather have been treading the boards any day, or night, than standing behind a shop counter.

Sam Fleming was, in fact, one of Ireland's leading step dancers. The talent ran in the family, for his sons and daughters were all great dancers, singers and instrumentalists. Together they did much for local charities and helped raise a few pounds for manys a good cause.

DANCING AND FITNESS!

Fleming had been a physical training instructor with the Royal Irish Fusiliers and was, himself, still a gymnast of quite some ability. He began classes in Ballymoney, Ballycastle and Coleraine and many a young fellow learned what real physical fitness was under the professor's watchful eye and rigorous instruction.

Ballroom dancing was popular in those days and Samuel Fleming ran classes for all comers in the upstairs department of a Coleraine building known as the Knitting Factory. That's when Speedy got to know him. He had become quite adept on the banjo, good enough to attract the attention of professor Fleming, who paid him a shilling a night to play in his seven piece dance band.

The professor was a first class impresario too. He seemed to know exactly what the public wanted in the line of entertainment, and he went out of his way to gave it to them. His minstrel troupe was a resounding success with the punters. When the whole cast of this old-tyme musical hall was on stage it made a colourful sight and a harmonious sound.

WHITE MINSTRELS!

The Fleming boys and girls rendered the melodic songs of Stephen Foster with sincerity and passion. The only thing missing, by comparison with more recent television efforts of this type, was the blackened faces of the players. Old man Fleming didn't allow this. He considered it degrading and offensive to coloured races. A gentleman at heart, he was always careful not to hurt the feelings of others.

That didn't mean he was some kind of kill-joy or stick-in-the-mud. Far from it. If you'd seen his 'corner men' at work you'd have realised that.

The corner men were Johnnie 'Dido' Clements, and Harry 'Joker' Anderson and it appeared that their job was to create as much mayhem as possible. With the entire cast on stage, doing their bit, the corner men took up position on either side of the stage and, in between songs, engaged in comic cross talk and plastered each other with cream cakes.

The Fleming minstrel troupe was renowned throughout N. Ireland and Donegal. Every year, in the springtime, their ten seater wagonette was hitched to a horse and off they went, bringing their brand of fun and entertainment to the towns and villages of Ulster.

From mid-June till mid-September they were on contract to Portrush Council's Entertainment Committee, giving three outdoor performances every day at Ramore Head.

BRIGHTON OF THE NORTH!

Back then, Portrush was referred to as the "Brighton of the North." The steam-ships 'Hazel,' and 'Fern,' arrived regularly from Scotland, bringing with them hundreds of happy holidaymakers.

Ramore Head, and the entertainment offered there by Fleming's minstrel troupe, was one of the big attractions.

If you could have stood at the back of the crowd, any day, you'd have witnessed almost every emotion known to man. At first, excitement as the stage burst into life.

Then humour, romance, sorrow and sympathy, as comedy sketches interspersed musical acts, magical shows and those perennial favourites, the songs of Stephen Foster.

The quality of those Ramore Head shows can be measured by the fact that, one afternoon, a member of a particularly large audience stepped up on stage, after the show, gripped the professor's hand and congratulated him on the show.

The kindly encourager was a Scottish miner named Harry MacLennon. That name will mean nothing to most readers, but when you realise that he was later to become Sir Harry Lauder, Scotland's most famous entertainer ever, you'll appreciate the importance of the moment to Samuel Fleming.

A sound and sincere friendship developed between the two men and they often corresponded with each other.

In one letter, Harry Lauder extended an invitation to the Fleming troupe to come and show off their talents in Scotland.

Great interest and excitement was engendered over the idea but, alas, the visit never materialised.

MUSIC!

Speedy became very attached to professor Fleming, who took a great interest in his musical potential. He kept advising Speedy to buy a saxophone which, he said, was the principal instrument of a good dance band.

One day, Speedy took the professor's advice. He stepped on the bus to Belfast, went to a music store, and bought himself a second hand silver saxophone. We're not told how much he paid for it, but when an ex-army bands-man looked it over he passed the observation that it must have come out of Noah's Ark!

Age and appearance didn't deter Speedy Moore. He was set on mastering this unique instrument and, what's more, he had his mother's blessing and encouragement.

Once he had managed to master the art of blowing the saxophone, he set about learning scales and simple tunes. At first the sounds that came from the bell of the instrument were a bit weird. Speedy was fascinated by his new found skill, the neighbours, however, were not so enamoured and soon the complaints began rolling into the local Council offices.

The Council wasn't against culture or musical advancement, but, at the same time, it did have to consider the privacy and sanity of its tenants. The outcome was a note to the budding young musician to hold his practice sessions as far away from the neighbours as possible.

BANISHED!

There was a big four acre field just outside town. In that field, behind a big stone, Speedy Moore learned most of his saxophone playing. It was a tough school for the weather wasn't always like a summer's day. However, being the determined character he is, Speedy stuck to his last and determined to master the instrument.

In course of time he was offered the sanctuary of a church hall and there he honed his musical skills, if not to perfection, at least to a level which was acceptable to the public. However, over the years, the saxophone has become a life long companion to him and he has become a master of the instrument. How many, down through those years, have been entertained and blessed by the sweet, melodic tones of Speedy and his sax.

Chapter Nine

THE PEN IS MIGHTIER!

It was in the latter years of his schooling that Speedy became aware of his ability with the pen. One of his school-teachers recognised the talent and encouraged him to develop it.

After he left school and started work, he began writing short pieces which were published in the local Coleraine Chronicle. His first big opportunity came, however, after a cycle run in the country, one sunny August afternoon.

Riding along a narrow mountain road, alone with his thoughts, his reverie was interrupted by an unusual sight. An old man, with a mop of white hair and a beard to match, was lying in the shade of a turf stack by the wayside. Speedy jumped off his bike, sprawled down beside him and learned that the old man's name was Peter Harper. The little white washed cabin, on the brink of the hill behind them, was where he was born. Through these fields he roamed as a boy, following his father's footsteps and learning how to be a shepherd, like him. Through these same fields he followed the sheep, as an adult, earning the bread to feed his own young family. They, in turn, roamed and romped and played in those fields too.

AWAITING THE GOOD SHEPHERD

But now they were all gone. Years before, he had buried his dear wife and a darling daughter. Now, with Christian patience, Peter awaited the call of the Good Shepherd, home to his sheepfold in glory. His earnest wish was that his remains be laid to rest alongside those of his wife and daughter.

Speedy and Peter became firm friends and, on return visits, Speedy would run errands for the old man, bringing whatever comfort he could to him.

One day, Speedy arrived as usual to keep old Peter company for a while. He found the cabin door shut and secured by a heavy chain and lock. Peter, of course, was no longer there. He had been taken away to the Workhouse and, horrible though that may sound, it was altogether better for a man as old and frail as he was. A feeble old man, living alone, could be a danger to himself.

Still, it must have been heart breaking for Peter to say farewell to the mountains and valleys he loved so much, and to leave behind the old homestead where he had known so much joy and happiness.

Saddened by these thoughts and events, Speedy returned home and composed the following lines in old Peter's dialect. He gave it a poignant title.

"The Pensioner's Elegy."

I'm a poor oul' man that's listenin'
For the Master's welcome call;
When it comes to pass, I'll be in the class
O' millionaires an' all.
It mak's nae difference who ye are
When ye reach the happy shore,
For it is true, there, me an' you
Will suffer niver more.

'Tis a gye long time since I was born
In eighteen an' forty three;
Count in yer mind an' ye will find
The proper age o' me.
An' I hae been honest doon the years
Which have had a rapid run,
I did nae harm nor caused alarm,
Ootside a bit o' fun.

I've had my wheen o' troubles, boy,
An' the worse one in my life
Was the sorrowin' day they carried away
The remains o' mae darlin wife.
But I know she's waiting there for me
Wae mae lovely daughter, Jane,
On a churchyard crest, their bodies rest
Near the borders o' Coleraine.

Noo mae one good freen's the clergyman,
An' a godly man is he,
There's no mony such wid bother much
Wae an' oul' done man lik' me.
But I hope he'll be rewarded soon,
Och, that I often pray:
He's young in life an' should hae a wife
Afore I go away.

Mae cabin consists o' two wee rooms,
An' I live there bae maesel,
I widnae gye its chimney
For the finest made hotel.
An' I hae a view o' the countryside
Frae my yard where I often stan'
An' the bonnie place, it bears the trace
O' the Master's mighty han'.

Noo, I'm tired o' yarnin' tae ye son,
An' the evenin's gettin' late:
Tae conclude our ta'k we'll hae a wa'k
The length o' the cabin gate.
'Tis soon I'll lay this cruel worl'
Tae meet my wife an' wane
An' on the churchyard crest we three will rest
Near the borders o' Coleraine.

Sadly, Peter's dying wish, for his remains to be laid beside those of his wife and daughter, was never granted. Like Mick, the buttermilk man, he was buried in the pauper's patch, a scant reward for a man who had lived such an exemplary life.

IN PRINT

When Speedy's beautiful and poignant poem was published in the Coleraine Chronicle, the then editor, Samuel Troy, signed it **W. 'Speedy' Moore**. Every story and article from Speedy's pen, since that day, has been signed in the same way.

That Speedy had a talent for story telling there was no doubt. He also had the ability to commit those stories to paper. The editor of the Chronicle was quick to spot this and, apparently, keen to encourage new talent. He asked Speedy to be on the lookout for any other little human interest stories he could find, like the one about Peter Harper. Speedy didn't have to be asked twice. He had an interest in people, an eye for detail and a nose for a good story. He went about the task with industry and enthusiasm and found it exciting and rewarding.

With this small amount of success under his belt, plus the approbation of the newspaper editor, Speedy realised that there was great scope for his writing talents.

The approval of the newspaper editor is not to be dismissed lightly. Who knows, the writings of Speedy Moore may never have seen the light of day had it not been for the foresight and encouragement of Samuel Troy. Readers of the 'W. Speedy Moore' column have a lot to thank him for.

WIDER HORIZONS

It didn't take Speedy long to discover that, when he was out fishing, there was a whole world of material opened up before him. Consequently, he began a series of articles on wildlife and nature.

He wrote about the pair of otters and their young in playful mood, sliding down a muddy slope, on their backsides, into Hegarty's Pool. He depicted that other expert fisherman, the heron, standing like a statuette carved from grey granite; and noticed the willy wagtail, dancing on the big stone in mid-stream.

He admired the red and white cow, licking her new-born calf with true motherly affection; and listened to the lark and the linnet singing high above his head in splendid rivalry. He painted word pictures of the beautiful flora and fauna that adorned the river banks; and readers could almost smell the scent of dandelions, buttercups and new mown hay.

But most of all he was attracted to the characters that roamed the country lanes and winding river banks. Some of these characters were fishermen, anglers, like himself. Their chief delight was the satisfaction of landing a 'Greenwell's Glory' or a 'Silver Doctor' over the nose of a proud salmon and waiting for the churn of the water as he took it with greedy boldness.

CHARACTERS GOOD AND BAD

A few of these riverside characters were not so sportsman-like. They wanted a salmon, or two, and had no scruples about how they got them. Not for them the skill of the cast, the patience of the play, or the satisfaction of coaxing a reluctant fish into the net. Fish on the bank was all that interested them, The more the merrier was their motto - and by any means - just as long as they weren't caught. While Speedy had no time for the motives or methods of these poaching rascals, he still found them interesting as subjects for his pen.

Then there were the characters who didn't fish at all. They had possibly never cast a line in their lives, but they liked to watch and be around those who did. They could loll against a ditch for hours on end, watching the anglers practice their skills, and their fishing tales were as entertaining as any man's. Many a line in Speedy's weekly newspaper column was filled with the yarns these old boys passed on to him.

Travelling the country, here and there, in pursuit of nuggets for the entertainment of his readers, brought Speedy into all kinds of company. A lot of it, alas, wasn't good.. At least it wasn't calculated to help him follow on the wise and sober pathway his mother had shown him. She was a temperance minded lady and had always been certain that her darling son would never become the victim of the booze trade.

THE DEMON DRINK!

It has to be said that drink, alcoholic beverage, wasn't as popular as it is today. The public house was still a place which only men frequented; it had yet to acquire the air of sophistication of modern times.

But booze was available in more places than in pubs and, unfortunately, like many another young man, Speedy was inveigled into trying it for himself. As he says himself *"The Devil's routine of way-laying youth is both cunning and baffling."*

Someone has said than *"No one starts out with the purpose of becoming an alcoholic."* Speedy Moore was to discover how true that statement is, and how much sorrow and hardship comes along with the abuse of alcohol.

At first, Speedy, persuaded to sip at a glass of beer, was almost inclined to spit it out again with revulsion. He couldn't imagine how people could sit all evening pouring pints of this foul tasting liquid down their necks, even less how they could derive any pleasure from it. However, like many another, he found out that alcoholic drink is an acquired taste, and once acquired, almost impossible to subdue.

Wherever Speedy went bottles of booze were produced as symbols of good will and courtesy. He actually came to believe that to refuse a glass of 'good cheer' was to be miserably unsociable. Yet, in the back of his mind were the memories of the sad histories of Hughie, of Dunlop Street, and a dozen other victims of the bottle he had heard of.

JUST A WEE GLASS!

However, friends kept telling him there was no harm in a wee glass from time to time. Speedy ended up quite confused. He says he was like the two young lads who met the dog at the gate of the big house.

One said to the other: *"Go ahead, open the gate, the dog is OK. Look, he's wagging his tail."*

"Yes he's wagging his tail all right, but look at those snarling teeth, and listen to that growl," replied the second boy.

They didn't know which to believe, the friendly wagging tail or the warning growls.

To avoid being looked upon as a spoil sport, a kill-joy and a social misfit, Speedy believed the signs given out by the friendly wagging tail and accepted his first glass of port wine. As it trickled gently down his throat he enjoyed its warming glow and its gentle stimulus. The first glass soon led to another, and then another. Before long he was sampling every brand and type of alcohol available.

THE SLIPPERY SLOPES

Slowly, but very surely Speedy Moore was slipping farther and farther away from the Christian teaching which had been instilled into him at his mother's knee, in Sunday School, and in the Boy's Brigade Bible Class. Along with the drinking he was smoking a packet of cigarettes every day, and of late, he had learned a few card games too. All these worldly vices were indulged, along with a crowd of other lads, every Sunday. That was probably the biggest insult of all to the faith in which he had been reared. What would his poor mother have thought - if she had known ?

He relates, with shame, what he refers to as *"The most embarrassing experience of my entire life."*

He had gone to a party with a few friends and had taken his banjo with him. As he strummed out lively tunes for the games and dancing, the boys and girls battered the floor with their feet. It was a happy, fun filled time.

Throughout the evening Speedy was constantly plied with glasses of wine, carried up to him on the stage. As quickly as they came, he downed them, without objection and the more he drunk the better he was able to strum the old banjo, or so he thought.

At the end of the evening he staggered down from the stage to the praise and congratulation of the organisers, one of whom had a bottle in his hand.

ONE FOR THE ROAD

"Well done Speedy, here, have a wee gin for the road," he said, and almost filled a large glass.

Speedy declined, but the man paid no notice and thrust the glass into his hand, insisting that his musical efforts were well worth a parting gargle.

After mixing the gin with a drop of lemonade, Speedy tried a mouthful. It wasn't bad, in fact it was quite nice, so he finished the glass and held it out for a refill.

"I'll show them I'm big enough to handle all the drink they fire at me," he though, puffing out his chest.

His 'manly' conduct resulted in him collapsing in a heap on the floor and going into complete darkness. Hours later he awoke with a terrible thumping in his head. It was like the battering of a sledge hammer.

Quite some time passed before he was able to recognise his whereabouts. When he did, he realised that he was on top of his own bed, in his own room. The entire sour contents of his stomach had, in his senselessness, gushed through every escape route of his unconscious, fully-clothed body. The stench was unbearable to his nostrils.

He realised that, in his drunken stupor, his friends had carried him home and dumped him on his poor mother. He shuddered. How could he face his mother in this disgraceful state? Why had they brought him home at all? Did they want to break her heart? Why hadn't they thrown him in a field somewhere, to sober up?

SHAME!

At last his mother came into the room. She was weeping bitterly. *"What do you think of yourself now?"* she asked between her sobs.

Speedy could only remain silent and weep with her. He was ashamed of what he had done.

"Our rent money has gone to the doctor," she wailed. *"We thought you were dead, at first, and one of our good neighbours rushed to get him. He removed your tie, opened your shirt neck, turned you face downwards and told us you were hopelessly drunk; you'd have to sleep it off."*

At that moment Speedy hated himself more than he had ever hated anything in his short life. As he lay there, in his misery, his mother wiped the tears away with the bottom seam of her white linen apron. Then she spoke again.

"Take those stinking clothes off you till I get them boiled and scrubbed. Then your sister Annie, who is crying her eyes out in the kitchen, will clean and fumigate this room."

She turned to leave the room, then stopped for one last word. *"I have the big bath tub ready for you in the scullery, and your clean clothes are airing by the fire."*

It was then that Speedy found the voice to cry out plaintively: *"Mammy, I'll never drink again ... I just couldn't, mammy!"*

If only lives could be changed by promises!

Chapter Ten

THE NIGHT HAWKS

Speedy's pursuit of the fun and pleasures this world had to offer, continued unabated. He started playing in a six piece, semi-professional group, "The Night Hawks."

Their name certainly suited them for their main engagements were dances and socials which, of course, were held at night and ran into the wee small hours of the morning.

The band consisted of the Fulton brothers, Alex, on piano and Jim keeping a steady beat on the drums. Sammy McLaughlin played violin and Stan Pattison hit the high notes on the trumpet. Speedy, himself, played banjo and saxophone.

The boys travelled all over the country which meant that, many a time they weren't home till dawn, or after it. Long sleeps throughout the daylight hours were not unusual.

Speedy was still scribbling away with the pen, in fact, he was now writing a regular column in the Chronicle, and it was well received by the paper's readership.

He was also earning a bit of a name for himself as a comedian. This new talent got him a place in a concert party which was in big demand. Between this, the dance band and the newspaper column he was doing quite well financially.

ON THE BROAD ROAD!

However, financial prosperity and the company he was keeping were drawing him steadily farther and farther away from the straight and narrow way. The promise he had made to his mother, when in the throes of drink, had long since been forgotten. Sadly, he had done that without the slightest qualm of conscience.

"I was weak, in every sense of the word, and figured that promises were made to be broken, even to the one who loved me so much," he confesses. *"I was now a man of the world and intended to have a good slice of it, away from that old-tyme religion stuff my mother and sister encouraged."*

His pursuit of pleasure and his growing addiction to drink, landed him in all sorts of predicaments. Looking back, many of those escapades have a funny side to them, but at the time, they were often costly.

"THIS IS THE B.B.C.!"

Once, years ago, the B.B.C. showed an interest in the kind of country concerts Speedy and his friends were engaged in. Speedy and a colleague had taken over the management of the concert group, so he wrote to the B.B.C. inviting them to came and have a look at their show.

It was agreed they would come to a concert in an Orange Hall, between Tobermore and Draperstown. Great preparations were made for the arrival of these important gentlemen from Belfast. A messenger was sent to Mrs. Lyle's farmhouse across the road, to borrow a couple of easy chairs, so that the B.B.C. men wouldn't have to sit on the old hard forms the rest of the audience used.

Prior to the concert Speedy had managed to borrow a set of tails, to make him look smart and professional. After all, this could be their big moment. Stardom was just over the horizon, they thought.

Just after the doors were thrown open for the audience, the doorman, a local, informed Speedy that two smart city-looking chaps had arrived and stepped out of a big black car. Rushing down to the door, Speedy greeted the strangers with a warm handshake and ushered them to the two easy chairs at the front of the hall.

When they had settled and were smoking Speedy's specially acquired, expensive brand of cigarettes, he excused himself for a moment, went to the

pay desk and took twelve shillings from the box. A messenger was
dispatched to Richardson's pub in Tobermore for a half bottle of old
Bushmills whisky, half a dozen Guinness and four glasses. They just
couldn't have men coming all the way from Belfast, to judge their efforts,
without offering them suitable hospitality. Besides, the liquid refreshment
might have a desirable influential effect on their judgement.

The show, that night, went as never before. Every artist sparkled and no
one in the audience clapped more heartily than the two gentlemen in the
easy chairs.

SURPRISE, SURPRISE!

Back stage, during the interval, they gladly accepted Speedy's hospitality, chasing down the whisky with a pint of Guinness a piece. Speedy,
excited and delighted at the way the two visitors were receiving the show,
poured himself a glass of Bushmills and was just about to knock it back
when the bombshell dropped.

"We're from the Ministry of Finance," said one of the men. *"We're here to
check your entertainment stamps!"*

Normally, they did use entertainment stamps all right, but since they
were away out in the wilds of the country, the doorman didn't think
anybody would bother about them. They were well and truly caught.

The result was a fine of £17 each, for Speedy and his management
partner, plus the cost of all that drink the two 'guests' had consumed so
sociably.

THE ROAD TO RUIN!

Drink, and its attendant curses was to dog Speedy for many more years.
He married, but that didn't change him. Even as his lovely daughter Nina
grew up and became aware of the curse that was destroying her father, her
pleas for him to stop fell on deaf ears.

Night after night he staggered home the worse for drink, falling into bed
in the clothes he wore, and waking up next day stinking and wretched.

Booze affected Speedy just like it affects any other man or woman who
becomes a slave to it. It undermined his work; it damaged his family; it
threatened his marriage; and it took away his respectability. Speedy Moore

was fast becoming dependant on drink. He was, in fact, turning into an alcoholic.

War service did nothing to change him either. If anything, it assisted him on his downward path. There's always plenty of drink about in the mess rooms and bars of an army camp and when, like Speedy, you're appointed batman to an officer, access to booze is even easier.

"SMILES AND TEARS."

The war passed and Speedy returned to his column in the Coleraine Chronicle. His writing was so successful, and so well received that, in 1972, he published a little book, "Smiles and Tears." It was immediately successful,, indeed, all the copies available to the public sold out in a very short time.

Speedy, not unsurprisingly, was gratified by the new found fame that being an author brought him. To celebrate his success he booked a big Portstewart Hotel for a party - a party with a difference. The meal was the best of good Irish stew and pig's trotters, and to wash it down there was plenty of whiskey. Indeed, it flowed like the river Bush in full spate.

At the end of the hooley Speedy, drunk as usual, was congratulated by all in sundry. He felt a proud fellow and, once again, scented success in the offing. But it wasn't to be. In no time at all he was as impoverished as ever. Every penny he made from the book had been ruthlessly squandered on drink. And the drink was continuing its subtle and malicious destruction of his life.

DR. JEKYLL AND MR. HYDE

Speedy records that in some ways he could have been described as a Jekyll and Hyde character.

"Outside the walls of the place I had the audacity to call home, I always wore a nice front. I didn't stagger or roll down the streets, and never used violence. In any situation my face could wrinkle into a sweet smile and I had a large repertoire of side splitting jokes. But in my own family circle I seemed to be a complete miss-fit and was never pleasant. All this was totally due to the hangovers caused by the devil's liquid."

He was still able to continue his newspaper column, although at times, thinking and concentration were difficult, to say the least. Fortunately, his wealth of experience, his vivid imagination, and his many contacts, from whom he could draw fresh resources, saw him through.

Most of the time his writing was done in the pubs he frequented. He couldn't face his colleagues in the newspaper office so, once a week he slipped in, submitted his copy, and slipped out again.

One morning, however, a note was waiting for him: "Ring Sean Rafferty, B.B.C.," it said.

"SPEAKING PERSONALLY"

When Speedy spoke to the well known broadcaster he was surprised when Sean said to him: *"You're next on the list for our Saturday morning radio programme 'Speaking Personally.' Can you come to Belfast on Wednesday, to record? Gloria Hunniford will be your interviewer."*

Something prompted him to say yes and a time was arranged, but after putting down the phone, he had certain misgivings.

First - he had nothing decent to wear to go to the B.B.C.'s elegant headquarters in Belfast. Secondly - he would have to be sober to talk on the wireless, but that was asking for some kind of a miracle. Third - would his befuddled mind react sensibly to Gloria's quick-fire and probing questions? And finally - what was he going to use for money to pay for the train fare from Coleraine?

Balanced against all those fears was the prospect that the broadcast might do well. If it did, some of Speedy's lost credibility might be restored. The fact that Sean Rafferty and Gloria Hunniford had selected him as an Ulster personality was great encouragement, but did they know about his drink problem? He wondered.

The Wednesday morning of the broadcast dawned and Speedy boarded the train for Belfast. His thread-bare brown suit had been dry cleaned in a hurry and he was sober as a judge. But sobriety brought its own problems. The shakes and dizzy-fits tormented him more than ever. How would he make it through this day? What would happen if he was offered a meal at broadcasting house? He couldn't have guided the food to his mouth let alone lift a cup of tea.

GETTING IT ON TAPE

Thankfully, no refreshments were offered and none were asked for. When the recording session was over Speedy breathed a great sigh of relief. He felt that Sean and Gloria were equally relieved. The interview had been a nightmare. Speedy, who always exuded confidence and was highly articulate found the whole experience a struggle. He was a complete bag of nerves. The stories and anecdotes that normally rolled off his tongue with consummate ease just wouldn't give themselves up. He had to stop and re-start again and again.

However, the engineers in the B.B.C. performed some kind of magic with the tapes and, when the broadcast went on the air, no-one ever knew that it had been born out of such tribulation. It was well received by all who heard it and Speedy could hold his head high again for a few days.

But the drinking went on unabated. The weekly consumption of alcohol had now gone far beyond what his pocket could afford and that introduced a far more serious aspect to his problems. Men and women who are addicted to drink must have it, somehow or other. If they can't afford it, they have to devise ways and means of getting it from others. This was the path Speedy, in his desperate state, was forced to follow.

BUDDY, CAN YOU SPARE A DIME?

It must have been a pathetic sight to watch a man with so much talent, so much ability, sitting on a bar stool, strumming at an old banjo in the hope that some of the other patrons would take pity on him and buy him a drink.

But that's how it was on many a night. Speedy would bang on the banjo and the glasses of whiskey would arrive beside him.

"Pub psychology is most mystifying," says Speedy. *"Those big-hearted lively druths didn't care what they spent on keeping me singing and strumming. Yet, if I had been hungry and had 'tapped' them for a meal to save my life, nine times out of ten I would have been refused."*

In the face of all this evidence Speedy still did not consider himself to be in need of help. A member of Alcoholics Anonymous once quizzed Speedy about his drinking habits. His questions were pointed, personal and to anyone else, except Speedy, who by this time was hardened, would have been embarrassing.

At the end of the question session the A.A. man didn't hesitate to inform Speedy that, in his considered opinion, he was an alcoholic and required treatment immediately.

Speedy stared at the man in amazement ....

"Me an alcoholic? Absolute rubbish! Is this man mad? Why, an alcoholic was a creature who lay in the stench of the gutter drinking meth' and other strange concoctions. Wasn't I an author and journalist. I could still write a weekly column, even if my hand did shake a bit and my mind got fuddled now and then. Chronic alcoholic indeed! There was no way I was going to accept that degrading title!"

PAT'S TALE

Speedy Moore's case seemed hopeless. Then one evening, coming out of a pub in Newmarket Street, Coleraine, he was accosted by Pat, an old friend, who asked if he could walk home with Speedy.

Pat was a former alcoholic. His drinking habits had almost killed him. An eight year boozing spree had separated him from his wife and family, his home and possessions, and earned for him the contempt of the whole community.

Forty-three times he had been treated for the problem but to no avail. Each time he was released he went straight back to the bottle. He lived in cow sheds, barns and stables. Sometimes he slept under the open canopy of heaven, the weather conditions mattering not, so long as he had a bottle of liquid comfort by his side.

Once, he knocked on the back door of a Macosquin farmhouse, hoping that the occupant would give him a drink to quench his thirst for alcohol. The door didn't open and, in his desperation, Pat went to lie down in one of the outhouses. There he spied a old tin with a couple of paintbrushes steeping in it. Instinct told him that here was his saviour and he looked more closely.

Sure enough, the tin contained methylated spirit. Pat removed the brushes, strained the liquid through an old rag and downed it, like it was lemonade.

As Pat walked Speedy home that evening he related his story and how, through the influence of Alcoholics Anonymous, he had been delivered from the curse that almost killed him. He also diagnosed Speedy an alcoholic and warned him, in all sincerity, of the consequences of his folly.

Speedy didn't like the message Pat was delivering but, eventually, he was persuaded to attend Alcoholics Anonymous

FACING THE TRUTH!

At the A.A. meetings Speedy learned that alcoholism doesn't confine itself to the gutter drunk. It is no respecter of persons, regardless of position, social standing, birth or background. Speedy, at last, realised he was addicted to the curse.

Night after night he sat and listened to the ghastly stories of other victims of alcohol. Many of these poor souls had been to the gates of hell and back, but they were committed to telling their stories in the hope that others would be warned of the inevitable consequences of drink abuse.

The meetings and the fellowship with others in the same situation did have a steadying influence on Speedy for a time. He sobered up, kept away from the pubs and walked the straight and narrow, one day at a time, pathway of the reformed alcoholic.

During this period of sobriety he met Jack, another reformed alcoholic. The two men chummed up together and gave each other mutual encouragement. They were possessed of a burning desire to stay sober and to change their pattern of living. They were not going back, they thought, to the old slavery that booze imposed. To help them achieve this better quality of life, they joined Alcoholics Victorious, a movement introduced to Northern Ireland by the late Dr. Bill Holley.

ALCOHOLICS VICTORIOUS!

Each Thursday evening Dr. Holley opened his own home to Alcoholics of all denominations. They sat together, ignoring their sectarian differences, united by their common bond. At an interval, Mrs. Holley served a welcome cup of tea accompanied by delicious home-baked fare. Then the meeting continued with the doctor reading from the Bible and preaching to the gathered assembly.

However, the precious gospel message from the good doctor's lips fell on deaf ears. Speedy was agnostic - bluntly agnostic! He couldn't accept the account of the virgin birth, nor of Jonah and the whale. The miracles of the Bible were all myths to him. Although, like many another drunk, he was always quick to quote the account of the 'water into wine' miracle to back up his thirst for alcohol. After all if Jesus could turn water into wine, to make a wedding feast go with a swing, it must be all right to indulge the stuff to your heart's content.

By this time Speedy's debts were completely out of control. He no longer answered knocks on his front door and he didn't walk along the main street, for fear of meeting someone to whom he owed money. His old system of borrowing £100 from one bank to pay back another was running out of steam, although he had begun to pay off some of his debts by weekly amounts. They were now showing signs of dwindling and, thanks to his sobriety, relationships at home were greatly improved.

UNFAIR TEMPTATION

In 1975 the all-Ireland Conference of Alcoholics Anonymous was held at Portrush. The Northern Ireland A.A. groups were delighted at the prospect.

As the great moment drew near it was agreed, both at A.A. headquarters, and in the editorial department of the Northern Newspaper Group, that no one was more qualified than a sober and reliable 'Speedy' Moore, to cover this prestigious event for the press. Speedy relished the prospect.

Who could have imagined that the coming of the Alcoholics Anonymous Conference to his district would have been the immediate cause for Speedy's further downfall.

Incredible as it may seem, at the dinner for distinguished guests on the opening night of the conference, a small sherry was offered to non-alco's, as an aperitif. The wisdom or otherwise of putting such temptation in front of a man who had almost been destroyed by drink, is debatable. In the event, Speedy succumbed, and that seemingly innocent action took him right back into the tunnel of darkness. Ironically, his friend Jack went 'off the rails' at the same time.

The following Monday morning Speedy was on his way to Gransha Hospital, outside Londonderry, a place he had managed to evade for years.

Three weeks later he was discharged, sadly, just in time to attend the funeral of a university lecturer, who had died as a result of excess drinking. This passing of such a brilliant man in pathetic circumstances spoke to

Speedy with power and conviction. As his pine coffin was lowered into the cold earth, he wept.

However, the tears were no sooner wiped away than Speedy was back in the very pub where they had drunk together. He was a hopeless case, due to follow his deceased friend if something wasn't done for him in a hurry.

"The big question was, what could anyone do for me when I had neither the ability nor the will-power to help myself?" he writes.

"I had looked forward so much to the arrival of 1976. It was going to be the year when I would be completely free of debt and happy and respectable again. But when January came I was drinking more constantly than ever."

At this low point in Speedy's life an extraordinary event took place. Once a month Speedy's invalid daughter attended a Divine healing service in Coleraine Presbyterian Church Hall. She was usually taken there by her husband but on one occasion he wasn't able to go and so Speedy was asked do the needful.

Everything went well until Speedy reached the church car park. However, as he was helping Nina from the car into the wheelchair his back gave a loud crack and he doubled in two with pain. He ended up a priority figure in the healing line with the minister and his assistant laying hands on him and praying for his speedy recovery.

Despite the agony he was in Speedy had no time for the men, or their prayers. His mind entertained only two thoughts - the danger of permanent disablement and the pub two streets away.

Before she passed on into glory, his daughter Nina maintained that the day the clergymen laid hands on her father was the same day God began to take an interest in his useless and ill-spent life.

He had a lot to do, but as Speedy was to discover, with the God of miracles, nothing is impossible.

Chapter Eleven

SLOWLY TOWARDS THE LIGHT

There are many links in the chain of a man's deliverance from any kind of addiction, and each of those links is equally essential. On the face of it, some of the links may seem greater, stronger and of more importance. However, with any single one of them missing, the chain would be incomplete and the deliverance impossible.

One of the links in Speedy Moore's deliverance from the power of alcohol began with a chance meeting. (**"And by chance there came down a certain priest that way" - Luke 10:31.**)

He had ventured out onto Coleraine's main street and, as usual, was a pathetic sight. His clothes were worn thin, his shoes had barely a sole in them and he, himself, was physically unwell. Drink was steadily, unremittingly, taking its toll. He shuffled along slowly, back stooped, head bent, doing his best to avoid every staring eye.

From across the street a powerful voice roared a cheerful greeting. The owner of the voice was Tom Hyde, another old pall of Speedy's.

TOM HYDE

Tom had been a leading member of one of Northern Ireland's well known Show Bands. He too had been rather fond of a drop of drink, from time to time and had indulged himself in the pleasures of the world for years.

But then, all of a sudden, the news came through to Speedy and his friends that Tom had given up the show band scene, said farewell to his dance hall friends, and got religion.

The boys couldn't believe it. They gave Tom a month to get over his religious fervour and be back under the bright lights where he belonged. But the month passed. Then two months, three months. A year went by and still Tom hadn't come back to those bright lights, as everyone in Speedy's social circle had expected. What satisfaction could he be getting from playing the piano at dull church functions and in wee mission halls?

Tom confronted Speedy in Coleraine's main street. *"Speedy,"* he said in a brisk commanding tone. *"Speedy, I want you to come to a meeting tonight in the Cloonavin Hotel. I'll pick you up at about a quarter to eight."*

"What kind of meeting is this?" Speedy asked warily.

"Oh, it's a meeting with a difference," he smiled. *"It's run by the Gospel Businessmen's Fellowship and the speaker is an old soldier like yourself ... Major William Batt .. you'll like him."*

Speedy shook his head and replied *"If it's a gospel meeting I don't want to be any part of it, and I've no notion of acting the hypocrite by going.*

Tom came closer and whispered in his lovely way: *"Speedy, old boy, you're not in good shape and it aches my heart to see you like this. I want to help you and I believe I can. Please, please come to that meeting tonight."*

Speedy was moved by this impassioned appeal and agreed to go - but under his own steam.

BACK IN THE ARMY!

He arrived at the hotel close to eight o'clock and made straight for the bar. There he stayed till almost the end of the meeting and then slipped into one of the back seats, just to show himself to Tom Hyde and prove that he had kept his promise.

At the end of the meeting he tried to slip out again but Tom was too quick for him. He grabbed Speedy the arm and, army fashion, marched him up to meet the speaker, Major Batt. The major the same military style and ordered Speedy to be seated. He then proceeded to pray loudly for the salvation of his soul and his deliverance from the demon drink. When he had finished the major wished him well and presented Speedy with a copy of the New Testament.

Speedy adjourned to the bar for further liquid solace and sat reflecting on the events of the past few minutes. How did the major know about his drink problem, and why did he have to make such a public fuss about it. It was very embarrassing and made Speedy highly indignant.

His financial situation was degenerating all the time. He was being chased by bill-collectors, bank managers, solicitors, summon-servers and law-enforcement officers. His debts were now so out of control that he had to drink to take his mind off them. And yet, the more he drank, the deeper into hell he was sinking. He was in an absolutely hopeless situation, and when sober, would turn the same question over and over in his mind: *"What am I going to do?"*

A DRASTIC PLAN!

One of the solutions he considered was suicide, and he had it all very carefully planned. He would drive to Williamson's stretch of the River Roe and wade into the deep pool. When the water filled into his thigh waders he would fall over, sink beneath the swirling waters, and drown. It would be the perfect accident and no stain of embarrassment or shame would be attributed to his family.

However, the suicide plan fell through. As he stood there in the river, almost thigh deep in water, Speedy found that the courage to 'end it all' didn't exist - at least not in him.

"What about the mysteries beyond the grave," he thought. *"Maybe there really is a God! Perhaps there is a heaven - and a hell! Perhaps I do need to make preparation for death!"*

He waded ashore, dismantled his fishing rod and hastened to the nearest pub for a double whiskey, all thoughts of suicide far behind him.

HOSPITAL AGAIN!

However, he still wasn't cured and the next stage was to have Speedy admitted to a community hospital. There, in an isolation ward, he was given special treatment for his alcoholism.

There wasn't much to do in the hospital all day, except go for walks around the wards. On one of these danders Speedy noticed an old, white-haired man, sitting by the side of his bed, reading a large book, through a magnifying glass. The old gentleman turned out to be the Rev. John Beatie, a retired Church of Ireland rector. He was ninety two years old.

Speedy just couldn't figure out why this man found the Bible so interesting. After all, in his long life and ministry, he must have digested the book a hundred times or more. What magnetic attraction did the 'old book' still have to attract his attention?

When Speedy, at last, got around to questioning his reverence about his addiction to the scriptures he was surprised by the reply. Leaving down his magnifying glass with a shaky hand, he paused, looked up, smiled benignly and spoke:

THE BOOK OF BOOKS!

"My dear boy," he said, *"Every time I read from this book I am the recipient of something beautifully new and inspiring. The message of the Bible fills me with solace and hope. This book is the rock of mankind and every one of us, including you, if I may say so, should get a footing on that rock. It will also guide us the way to everlasting with our heavenly Father."*

A conversation with the Rev. John ensued in which he expressed his desire to shake of this mortal coil and to ascend into the presence of the saints.

"At ninety-two the flesh is a heavy burden to carry, 'Speedy.' But I'm consoled by the knowledge that one day soon I will hear the Master's final call and go home to glory land, to meet my Saviour face to face."

"Oh that will be, glory for me!
Glory for me, glory for me.
When by his grace I shall look on his face,
That will be glory, be glory for me!"

"THE SEED IS THE WORD"

That evening Speedy walked up and down the isolation ward weeping bitterly. The Reverend John had planted a good seed in his heart; it was taking root and bearing fruit very quickly. As the hours ticked away the more convicted of sin Speedy became. He thought of his destiny - sixty-four years old and at the end of his tether - a write off - finished!

His mind travelled back over the years to the hearth side in the house where he grew up in Killowen. He could see his mother, her face toil worn and wrinkled with trial and sorrow, sitting in the glow of the gas light, reading from the Bible.

At her knee Speedy had learned the stories of Jesus as a boy, as a man and as the Saviour. He could hear her gentle voice recount again the story of the cross and saw the Saviour hanging there, dying for him, a needy sinner.

He contemplated these Biblical scenes for a while, then, barely hopeful that his desperate prayer would be heard, he cried out to God for mercy, collapsed into bed and fell fast asleep. He never stirred till morning.

THE DAWNING OF A NEW DAY!

Next morning he awoke strangely relaxed, feeling as he had never felt before. A Gideon New Testament lay on the table beside the bed and he felt compelled to reach out for it. Opening it at random his eyes fell upon the invitation of Jesus in Luke's gospel: *"Ask, and it shall be given unto you; seek, and ye shall find; knock, and it shall be opened unto you." (Luke 11:9.)*

Tears filled his eyes as he read the Master's invitation. It was a Sunday morning in April and as he stood at the window, looking out over the countryside with it's beautiful coat of springtime green, for the first time in many years he was aware of the handiwork of God.

For many years, since he had first started to work, Speedy Moore had turned his back on the old-time religion. He had no time either, for those who professed salvation by grace.

"These people who called themselves Christians," he thought, "are just a bunch of hypocrites. They're kill-joys, mean, miserable and detestable."

But as he stood at that window he realised that the God of these Christians was working in answer to their prayers. Many of these people, whom Speedy despised and rejected, had been earnestly crying to God in their prayers for the salvation and deliverance of this drink besotted journalist.

THE JOY OF THE LORD

'Twas a great day, that first new day as a Christian. Speedy hardly knew what was wrong with him - or more properly - what was right with him.

A great burden had lifted from his shoulders; a strange peace filled his heart, and he was consumed with the joy of the Lord.

The next morning, Monday, he picked up his old banjo and went round to the Rev. John Beatie's bedside. When Speedy told him of his new found faith then old man was overjoyed.

"Looks like we're going to meet on the Heavenly shore after all, 'Speedy.' Just you keep trying. The Lord loves a man who keeps trying," he said.

Speedy held the banjo up in the air and replied: "I know only two gospel tunes - 'The Old Rugged Cross,' and 'Amazing Grace.' I'm waiting on your request, sir."

"I think 'Amazing Grace,' would be very appropriate," came the soft reply.

Effortlessly and gently, Speedy picked out the sweet old air on the strings of the banjo ....

"Amazing grace, how sweet the sound,
That saved a wretch like me.
I once was lost but now am found,
Was blind but now I see."

Never had the words of John Newton's best loved hymn been more appropriate. Its message and its testimony fitted the case of Speedy Moore perfectly.

At the end of the song Speedy laid down his banjo and the old reverend gentleman clapped his frail hands in appreciation of the music. It was the last gospel praise he was to hear on this earth. Two hours later the Rev. John Beatie, saint, servant and soldier of Christ, was called to his eternal reward. To the end he had witnessed a good confession of faith and pointed men and women to his Saviour. I wonder if, in glory, he has any knowledge of what a great trophy of grace Speedy Moore turned out to be.

THE FIRST BIG TEST!

That Speedy has turned out to be a trophy of grace is undisputed. However, it hasn't been all plain sailing since that wonderful moment of conversion.

Almost immediately he faced the maximum temptation possible to a man of his background.

It was the afternoon of the Rev. John Beatie's funeral when a car drew up outside the hospital where Speedy was being treated. The driver was a publican whose premises Speedy had frequented regularly over the years. In an affable manner he invited his old friend outside.

Opening the boot of his car he gestured to Speedy with a wave of his arm. Speedy's eyes almost popped out of his head at the sight that greeted him. There were bottles of booze galore!

"Just a wee gift from some of my customers, staff and me," said the publican, *"just to prove that we haven't forgotten about you."*

Beads of sweat oozed from Speedy's forehead and trickled down his face. Then an inner voice said *"Take it man, and drink it. Go on, have a good time. Sure you can get converted again anytime."*

Thankfully, God's Holy Spirit gave Speedy the grace to resist the temptation so thoughtlessly placed in front of him. The publican couldn't quite believe his ears but, at least had the sense not press the issue. As he drove off, shaking his head in confusion, Speedy lifted his heart in a silent prayer of thanksgiving.

CONFESSING HIS FAITH

Next day Speedy took his pen and wrote to his friend Jack, who was in a different hospital. It was a simple letter, recording the hours of agony before casting himself on the mercy of God, and the glorious experience when the light of the gospel finally shone into his soul. He concluded:

"Jack, I pray and trust you will strive to find the same salvation, for only God has the answer to our problem."

On the afternoon of the day he was discharged from the community hospital, Speedy went along to visit his old friend. As he entered the ward where Jack lay, the sight that met his eyes filled him with joy. Jack had the open Bible in his hands, and the radiant smile on his face indicated that his search for peace and reconciliation was over.

For genial Jack the fog had lifted just in time. Next morning he was found asleep in the Lord. Speedy wept at the news of his old friends' passing but was consoled by the knowledge that, one day, they would meet again in the great Mansion in the sky.

Chapter Twelve

GO TELL SOMEONE ABOUT JESUS

At sixty-four years of age Speedy Moore had a lot of catching up to do. The Bible, the book which had enjoyed an honoured place in the home he grew up in, had been neglected by him for years. With enthusiasm and hunger he began to read it again and soon discovered that the Bible is truly the wonderful *Word* of God.

The Bible is a *simple* word. The message of the gospel isn't difficult to understand when approached with a trusting heart and an open mind.

The Bible is also a *sure* word. It can be taken at its face value. Compare that with the words of men.

The Downing Street Declaration of December 1993 was announced jointly by British Prime Minister, John Major and Irish Prime Minister, Albert Reynolds. It was meant to bring an end to the violence in strife torn Northern Ireland, and introduce a new era of peace.

The document, which contains more words that God's moral law, the ten commandments, was described immediately by one BBC political correspondent as *"A Study in Ambiguity."* For weeks and months afterwards politicians and commentators argued and debated about what the words of the document really meant. As the dust gathers on the fading pages of that Declaration, clarification is still being sought. Not so with the Word of God. What God says in his Word, He means - and he means what He says.

God's Word is a *sustaining* word. When Speedy Moore came to the Lord the town of Coleraine was stunned by the news. Many of his old friends gave him the usual week, two weeks, or a month before he'd be back in the pubs again. Others did their best to place temptation in his way; hoping to see his downfall. But, over the years, Speedy has learned the value of that precious promise of Jesus: *"I will never leave thee, nor forsake thee."* (Heb. 13:5.) That word of God has sustained him continually.

But then God's Word is also a *steadfast* word. That promise *"I will never leave thee, nor forsake thee,"* sustained Speedy, not only in the early days of his new found faith, but ever since. With many another, he can declare with confidence and conviction that the Bible is truly an everlasting book. Its truths and promises are as dependable today as when they were penned by those holy men of old.

PRAISE THE LORD!

Speedy's study of the Word of God eventually brought him to the book of Psalms where these words struck him with great power:

"Praise God with the sound of the trumpet; praise him with the psaltery and harp. Praise him with the timbrel and dance: praise him with stringed instruments and organs. Praise him upon the loud cymbals: let everything that hath breath praise the Lord." (Psalm 150.)

The exhortation set him thinking about how he could contribute to the worship and praise of God. The last place he had played the saxophone was in a lounge bar. As usual, drink had been taken that night and the instrument, forgotten in an alcoholic haze, had been left behind. When Speedy went back next day to collect it, the pub was a different place. A terrorist bomb had reduced it to a mass of smouldering rubble.

However, since there was still drink available, and it was flowing freely, the saxophone was forgotten.

CUTTING HIS TEETH!

Sometime later Speedy was invited to give the testimony of his conversion at the Society Street Mission Hall, in his own home town, Coleraine. It would be fitting to include some music, he thought, so he rang the proprietress of the bombed out bar to enquire about the whereabouts of his precious saxophone, not expecting very good news. To his surprise and amazement, she informed him that the instrument had 'miraculously' survived the blast.

On the evening of the meeting he was joined at the front of the hall by none other than Tom Hyde. As Tom tickled the ivories and Speedy blew the saxophone, it was like a return to the old days for them both.

This time, however, they were in God's service and, as the soothing strains of "I Need Thee Every Hour," filled the packed hall, both men's eyes were moist with tears.

A BOOKIE'S CERT?

Many people in the town of Coleraine rejoiced at Speedy Moore's conversion. Others, alas, mocked it. The betting in the pubs that Speedy used to frequent was heavy.

"Three to one Speedy will be back on the bottle before Saturday," some said.

"Four to one he'll be back within a fortnight," said others. *"He just couldn't stay away, pubs are his whole life."*

But the gamblers underestimated the saving grace of God. They didn't realise that God can do anything but fail. He had made a good sound job of Speedy Moore, spiritually, mentally and physically. As time would prove, it was to be a lasting job.

EARLY ENCOURAGEMENT

Thankfully, there were many who made it their business to encourage the former alcoholic. One evening a neatly dressed young businessman came to Speedy's door, handed him a parcel, and left with hardly a word of explanation.

The parcel contained a beautiful, large print Bible - Speedy's first - and inside the front cover was the inscription: *"Enquire within about everything."* It was signed by Rodney Lyle.

Naturally, Speedy was touched by this thoughtful Christian gesture and, in time, he and Rodney Lyle became firm friends, with the young man fulfilling the role of spiritual mentor.

Some months after his conversion Speedy found himself in a mission hall in Garvagh, a small town in County Londonderry. He was there to photograph and interview a gospel group from Ballymena, for his news-paper.

T.B.F.

When the job was done and he was about to leave the hall Tommy Thompson, well known businessman and promoter of God's work, way-laid him. He invited Speedy to return to the hall on the following week and give testimony to what the Lord had done for him.

Speedy couldn't say 'Yes,' and didn't want to say 'No.' He just stood there until Tom Thompson's persistency paid off and he agreed to the request.

But as he made his way home his mind was troubled. Standing on a concert stage, telling jokes by the dozen, was no problem to Speedy. He was well used to it. But standing up there in front of rows of saints was a different matter.

"What will I say to those people on Tuesday evening?" he kept asking himself over and over again.

He sat writing for hours at a time but again and again, after only a few paragraphs, the paper was screwed up into a ball and thrown in the waste basket.

The newspaper advertisement on Tuesday morning, announcing his appearance at the meeting, did nothing to ease his agony.

Picking up the phone he began dialling the number of the people in Garvagh, to tell them he hadn't the guts to go through with the testimony.

He had heard that some of his former pub mates were planning to be at the meeting, just for a laugh at him. But as his fingers picked out the numbers on the telephone dial, the words of Psalm 40 and verse 2 came into his mind. *"He brought me up also out of an horrible pit, out of the miry clay, and set my feet upon a rock, and established my goings."*

Weeping like a child he dropped the phone and muttered to himself: *"God, who saved me from the lake of fire, will surely see me through a simple period of testimony."*

And He graciously did. Afterwards T.B.F. Thompson remarked *"God has plans for you, Speedy!"*

Even the great businessman couldn't have foreseen what great things were in store for the reformed alcoholic.

INSTANT SUCCESS!

Next morning a telephone call from a clergyman invited him to come and give his testimony at a weekly after-church rally. He had heard good reports of Garvagh and wanted his people to hear Speedy Moore for themselves, first hand.

He readily agreed, much more confident now, after his 'triumph' at Garvagh. When he arrived at the meeting, however, he was to learn a valuable lesson, that even in God's work, there are those who will use you for their own ends, if they can get away with it.

The minister had advertised the meeting widely, emphasising the fact that Speedy was a former alcoholic. This paid dividends for, on the night of the meeting, instead of the twenty or so souls who usually attended, the hall was packed.

"For this splendid turnout we must thank God," said the minister, as he warmly welcomed Speedy. He led him into a small room at the rear.

After prayer, he studied Speedy closely and then enquired: *"How long is your testimony?"*

Speedy informed him it would take about twenty minutes to tell his story. The minister strongly suggested that it should be cut down to about five or seven minutes; he had a lengthy message to deliver and another meeting to go to after this one.

This disappointed Speedy and, being a temperamental type, he was on the verge of walking out. Thankfully, the Lord enabled him to resist the temptation to quit, and the meeting was a great success. But, as Speedy himself says: *"This was only the first of many knocks I was going to take in my Christian walk."*

"JESUS IS ALIVE!"

By the grace of God he has walked on with God now, for over eighteen years. At eighty-two years of age he's an inspiration to anyone who loves the Lord. As I sat with him recently, in his Coleraine newspaper office, his eyes danced with heavenly light as he said to me: *"Jesus is alive, James. He's a wonderful Saviour, and He's done so much for me!"*

In eighteen years Speedy's testimony and new found faith in Christ have taken him all over the country, and to other countries too. He has stood on platforms with the great and the famous from all over the world. Names like Chuck Colson, William McCrea, Sir Harry Secombe, Ian Paisley and Sam Workman are all among his list of personal friends.

Great have been the experiences, too. Once, in a small Baptist church in Lerwick, in Shetland, a lady asked him what had been the nicest thing ever to happen to him. He thought for a moment and then reflected on what the Lord had done for him in delivering him from drink.

SURE AND STEADFAST!

Years ago he had been assigned to cover the annual inspection of the Boys Brigade, in his home town. As he stood there, down at heel and suffering the rigours of drink, he thought back to his own childhood and youth. As a shiny faced lad, he too had marched in a neatly pressed suit, with brightly burnished belt buckle and snow-white lanyard, to a Sunday dedication service.

As he watched these similarly clad lads, on a Sunday afternoon, in Coleraine, he wondered where he had gone wrong. Many of his old Boys Brigade companions had done well in this life. They had adhered strictly to the principles of the B.B. and had achieved happiness and success. And here was he, a down at heel reporter, with little to show for his life of constant toil.

However, years later, a reformed and delivered Speedy Moore was honoured by that same B.B. Company he had reported on years before. He was asked to act as their Inspecting Officer and was delighted to accept. What a thrill it was for him to take the salute as those young men marched past in strict formation.

"That Ma'am," he said to the silver haired old lady, as they sat and supped tea after that meeting in Shetland. *"That Ma'am, is the nicest thing that ever happened to me!"*

THE SMALL SCREEN

Over the years Speedy has had his share of positive publicity, as a result of his conversion. He has appeared on the television programme *"Insight,"* and was given a full twenty-five minutes, all to himself, to tell how God had saved him from disaster.

Then, some time later, he had the privilege of appearing alongside Sir Harry Secombe in *"Highway."* Again he had the joy of testifying to God's wonderful saving grace and power. Letters of congratulation and encouragement came from all over the country and he had the joy of pointing one of the writers, an alcoholic, to his Lord.

Being a handyman with the pen, Speedy put together and published a booklet on his testimony, entitled *"To God be the Glory."* His personal and secret wish was that:

"If just one solitary wretch reads this narrative, by chance, and is delivered from the curse and horrors of alcohol as I knew them, then every hour I spent writing it would be justified."

Well, not just one, but many former sinners could point to Speedy's booklet as the starting point on their road to salvation. Perhaps the most astonishing of all was Jim.

A SERIOUS CASE

A chronic alcoholic of the worst type, Jim was a constant source of torment to himself, to his lovely wife, and to his six children.

One morning he headed off on another drinking spree, taking the car with him. Later that day, strongly under the influence of drink, he drove down a busy street and hit another vehicle.

Knowing himself to be in the wrong he kept driving, trying to escape the penalty for his wrong. The police were alerted and, after a furious car chase the hit-and-run driver was cornered. He wasn't about to surrender easily though; a fight ensued in which a police officer was assaulted.

Jim was in serious trouble this time and as he sat in a police cell overnight, to cool off and sober up, he realised that his folly would cost his family dear. But what could he do?

Next morning, as he left the police station, a Christian police inspector handed him a copy of Speedy's booklet. In truth, the inspector had no great expectations but he has to be credited with having the wisdom and courage to sow the seed.

Back at home, the alcoholic, with shaking hands and trembling heart, read the story of how Speedy had been delivered from the same problem as his own. A glimmer of hope entered his soul.

REGRET

A few days later he returned to the police station, expressed his regret for what had happened, and apologised. Then he asked to speak to the Christian inspector who had given him the booklet.

The inspector was in court, he was told, prosecuting a number of cases. Walking across to the Court House, he sat waiting until four o'clock, the time the court business finished.

In tears he pointed to the booklet and blurted out to the inspector: *"How can I find the same peace as the writer of this .... can you help me?"*

The police inspector, a godly man, knew exactly how to help Jim. Opening the Word of God, he showed Jim that, just like every other man ever born, he was a sinner. He showed him, too, that Christ Jesus came from Heaven's glory and died at Calvary to take away man's sin. Jim could come into the experience of sins forgiven, simply by confessing his need and calling upon Jesus to be his Saviour.

CONVICTED AND CONVERTED

There, in the Court House, Jim bowed his head, confessed his sin and received Jesus Christ as Saviour and Lord. It was probably the most glorious conviction ever witnessed in that court house. Today, Jim is fully engaged in the Lord's service and has seen his wife and family come to the Saviour too.

As Speedy told me that story, it wasn't with any sense of vain pride or worldly satisfaction. He was just overjoyed that the Lord was pleased to use his simple testimony in the deliverance of another needy soul.

REFLECTIONS!

All new believers suffer discouragements and Speedy was no different, as has already been seen. It's sad though that some of those discouragements came, not just from those who opposed his conversion, but from those who welcomed it too.

For the first few weeks after the news raced around town that Speedy Moore had 'got religion' there was jubilation among the saints. They welcomed him with open arms; invited him into their homes; showered hospitality upon him, and listened again to his conversion story.

A HELPING HAND

However, after a few weeks, once the novelty had worn off, they seemed to forget about him. He received few invitations and felt very lonely again. About this he says:

"I needed somebody to steady my Christian walk and to keep me on the track, but a lot of them forgot about me. So I just looked up and I depended upon God. And God looked after me for he says 'I will never leave thee, nor forsake thee.' "

And on how Christians should behave towards alcoholics he has this to say.

"An alcoholic is a person who needs a lot of attention and care, and a little bit of love. The finger of scorn is often pointed at him. Bricks are thrown at him, even sometimes by Christians, because they think an alcoholic is almost impossible to rescue. But he's not.

They should be praying for him. They should be going and seeing him and talking to him. He might be a bit awkward, he might be a bit obstinate, but they will get through if they persist.

The alcoholic wants a way out and he'll take any way out to get away from the Devil's chains. Their job, as conscientious Christians and servants of God Almighty is to try and take those chains from him."

But even after conversion, those who have been delivered from alcoholism need care, attention and encouragement. Just because a man or woman becomes a Christian doesn't mean that the Devil gives up and leaves them alone. Far from it! The temptation of booze is still there and Satan will see that it is placed in front of the new born saint at every opportunity.

"LEAD US NOT INTO TEMPTATION"

A few years ago Speedy went to visit his daughter and son in law, in Canada. It was Christmas time and they had a bit of a do for a few friends and colleagues from work. There was a large dish of cocktail punch on hand for the guests, with glasses and a neat little ladle for filling them.

Speedy played the banjo for a while, to entertain the guests and they all enjoyed his music and singing. Singing and banjo playing is thirsty work, so it was suggested to Speedy that he should have a glass or two of this mild punch. *"It'll not do you any harm,"* they said. After a bit more music and singing Speedy left the banjo down and an unseen voice said *"Go ahead, try a glass or two of that. It'll never do you a bit of harm."*

He made to get up to help himself to some of the punch when he was physically pushed back down again, by an unseen hand, a hand he could not resist.

"I'll never forget that incident as along as I live," he told me with tears of gratitude in his eyes.

In such marvellous ways God has looked after Speedy Moore all these years, and used him to the blessing of multitudes. Bear in mind that he's now a man of eighty-two years of age. He didn't come to know the Lord until he was sixty-four, so what has been achieved for the Saviour is all the more remarkable.

Remarkable, too, are the circumstances that surround some of the opportunities he has had to witness for his Lord.

UP TO THE WHITE HOUSE

Speedy was sitting watching television one day when who came on to the screen, playing a saxophone, but the newly elected president of the United States, Mr. Bill Clinton.

Being a sax player himself this interested Speedy. He had just produced a new cassette tape of gospel music featuring himself on banjo, Hawaiian guitar and saxophone. A friend of his, Margaret Scott, who now lives in Ballycastle, was sending six of these tapes to friends in America. Margaret had spent her life in the U.S.A., had done very well, and had now come back home to her birthplace, to retire.

Speedy decided to give Margaret an extra tape and asked her to send it to the president, which she did. Along with it went a nicely typed letter, giving an outline of Speedy's life and conversion, pointing out that Margaret had enjoyed a full and prosperous life in the States, and wishing Mr. Clinton God's blessing in his term of office.

LONG DISTANCE

Some weeks later, on a Sunday afternoon, Margaret's telephone rang, and when she answered it, the caller announced herself as President

Clinton's secretary. After establishing that it was indeed the president's secretary, and not someone trying to pull her leg, the caller said that the great man was sitting beside her and would like to speak to her.

The president pointed out that he was a Baptist and had been raised on these familiar old gospel tunes. Speedy's tape had been a real inspiration to him and, indeed, as he played it on the loud-speakers, he had blown along with it on is own saxophone.

Thus, the first ever Presidential telephone call to Northern Ireland was prompted by Speedy Moore's testimony in music.

THE KING'S BUSINESS

When you step into the reception office of the Northern Newspaper Group these words, neatly framed on the wall, confront you.

This is a printing office.
Cross-roads of civilisation.
Refuge of all the arts
against the ravages of time.
Armoury of fearless truth
against whispering rumour.
Incessant trumpet of trade.
From this place words may fly abroad,
not to perish as waves of sound,
but fixed in time.
Not corrupted by the hurrying hand,
but verified in proof.
Friend you stand on sacred ground.
This is a printing office!

Speedy is still busy in that office every working day. He told me that every time he talks to the boss about laying down his pen and retiring, he chases him.

His weekly newspaper column *"People and Places,"* is published every week and enjoyed by thousands. And almost simultaneously with the publication of this book, his own novel *"The big Brae,"* comes on to the book-shelves. There's little doubt that it'll be a best seller.

Speedy Moore isn't a man for settling down by the fireside with slippers and a book. He prefers the great outdoors of the countryside in which he grew up, and when the occasion presents itself, he's still very keen on the fishing.

He admits, though, that his home is a changed place now, especially for his dear wife. Sometimes, in the evenings they sit together, just the two of them, and reminisce over old times. He's doing his best, he says, to try and make up for the years the locust has eaten. There, truly, is the sign of the grace of God in a man's life.

A NEW ADDICTION

But above all he wants to witness for his Lord. That gives him his greatest delight. Someone has suggested that, whereas Speedy was once addicted to alcohol, he is now addicted to Christianity. He pleads guilty to the charge.

"The word addiction covers a lot of things and certainly I'm addicted to serving the Lord. And you don't have to go into the pulpit and preach sermons to serve God. I do it as I walk up and down the street every day."

THE JOKER!

And Speedy is very fond of using his sense of humour in his day to day witness. When the Lord saved him he wondered if he would have to say farewell to his sense of fun. So he asked the Saviour about it.

"Lord when you created me you gave me a sense of humour. Now that I'm in your family do I have to forget about that sense of humour. The message came back almost immediately. 'No!' you don't forget about your sense of humour. Salvation is not a dull thing."

So, when he accompanies someone like Victor Hutchinson, the accordion player and singer, to a gospel meeting, Speedy introduces a touch of humour to the proceedings. He has an endless fund of funny stories and he's not slow to take a hand out of his fellow musicians or speakers. But back of all the fun, in his more serious moments, he's eternally grateful for the miracle of grace wrought in his life.

"If ever a man discovered God," he confesses, *"that man was me. I was too big, too clever to believe in that Good Book, or to believe in God. But only God, Himself,*

could have saved me from disaster. I had tried everything, mental homes, hospitals, organisations. I was even in a therapy class for backward children, making wee baskets, to try and get me away from that curse, that devil's liquid, alcohol."

FINAL TESTIMONY!

As I sat listening to Speedy I was aware of being in the presence of a man who has had a great burden lifted from his shoulders. Even as he spoke I could see the relief on his face and hear it in his voice.

"The only time that I found the peace and the joy which passes all understanding was the Sunday morning in April 1976, when the lovely Lord Jesus Christ came along and said 'Wilt thou be made whole, Speedy?' This in answer to the prayers of the Christians whom I despised. I said 'yes' and here I am today so happy that I can't believe this is me."

His closing words struck me forcibly. I've seldom seen such enthusiasm for the Saviour in any man. But it was there and Speedy Moore made no attempt to hide it.

"Jesus is very much alive James, believe me!"

'Beyond the big brae.